For People Like Us

For People Like Us

God's Search for the Lost of Luke 15

Luuk van de Weghe

Foreword by Justin Brierley

WIPF & STOCK · Eugene, Oregon

Wipf & Stock
An Imprint of Wipf and Stock Publishers
199 W. 8th Ave., Suite 3
Eugene, OR 97401

www.wipfandstock.com

PAPERBACK ISBN: 978-1-6667-5650-0
HARDCOVER ISBN: 978-1-6667-5651-7
EBOOK ISBN: 978-1-6667-5652-4

02/14/23

To my best friend, Sandy. I am glad that this is not a marriage book, because all the marriage books we read were wrong. At least, they were wrong about what I should have expected. Being married to you has been so much better, so much richer, than any of those books led me to believe was possible. I have no doubt that this book would never have been written without you.

Contents

Foreword

A FEW YEARS AGO I had the privilege of spending some time with Luuk and his family in the small town where they live, among the mountains, shores, and forests of the Pacific Northwest. Their beautiful rural location, where industries such as fishing and logging have been part of life for generations, is the kind of place that puts you in touch with nature and with the local inhabitants. People know the value of hard work, and everyone knows everyone else.

That's a good background to be able to enter the culture of Jesus as he tells stories about shepherds, neighbors, farmhands, land owners and sons who choose to work hard . . . or decide to run away from their responsibilities.

What I most appreciate about Luuk is that he is an excellent Bible scholar but not the sort who lives shuttered away in an ivory tower (in fact he built the house he lives in from the trees that grow around him). Luuk has his head both in the original Greek texts of the New Testament but also in the real daily lives of a working community on his doorstep.

When Jesus (someone who also knew the value of a hard day's labor) told his stories about sheep, coins, and sons, he was talking to real people about scenarios and relationships they would have been familiar with. However, the passage of time, the fact that most of us don't live in rural communities any longer, and our over-familiarity with these stories can sometimes stop us from appreciating their radical message and the way they would have impacted their original audience.

Within these pages you will find a scholarly understanding of these stories that freshly illuminates their meaning. In particular I find Luuk's exposition of the story of the lost sons (yes, there are two of them!) one of the best I have ever encountered. Here you will discover context, background, and textual analysis that highlights the culture, humor, and shocking challenge of the stories that Jesus told. It is not without reason that Charles Dickens reputedly described the story as the "finest short story ever written." Not only does Luuk bring out new dimensions that we may have missed, but in doing so he points to the brilliance of the storyteller himself and how extraordinary his prodigal love is.

Most importantly, Luuk brings home why these stories are about "people like us." We are all lost sons or daughters—whether we end up being lost "away" or "at home." That the God of the universe was willing to lose his own son in order to find us again is the best news we could ever hope to hear. This book will help you to understand why the story of the father and his two sons was placed at the center of Luke's Gospel and why it should always be at the center of our understanding of who God is. For in the end, this is a story not about a prodigal son, but a prodigal father, who loves us more than we can ask, understand, or imagine.

Justin Brierley
Speaker, broadcaster, author of *Unbelievable? Why After Ten Years of Talking with Atheists, I'm Still a Christian*, and Theology and Apologetics Editor at Premier Christianity

Introduction

Is God for me? Few questions are more important. To put it in perspective, think about a single paper cup. Just a regular, eight-ounce cup like the one on my desk by the window in my office, which is approximately two hours outside of Seattle by combination of car and ferry.

From here, I see a large container ship moving along the horizon of the Strait of Juan de Fuca, likely bound for the Seattle port. This strait constitutes the entryway into a beautiful set of bays and lagoons outlined by tree-covered peninsulas, creating tentacles of deep, peaceful blue. The entire region is named after this squid-like body of water, the Puget Sound, which encompasses a thousand square miles. Now imagine that cup on my desk. Suppose I were to take that cup and fill it with some water from the Puget Sound. Then, suppose I grab another cup, doing the same. Imagine I did this again and again and again, setting up my cups of water along the Puget Sound shoreline, one at a time, somehow draining the Puget Sound of its water.

This would be roughly equivalent to draining Europe's Lake Geneva or the Dead Sea. The task is seemingly inconceivable. It would take approximately five hundred trillion cups of water—that is, five hundred thousand cups multiplied a billion times.

Continue to imagine those cups. Now, imagine me repeating this experiment four hundred million more times. More times than there are people living in the United States. By the time I finish, I would have scooped up thirty times the amount of water of all the oceans of the world. If we imagine those cups in their totality, we have an approximate visual of how many stars there are in the known universe. There are approximately thirty times more stars in the universe than there are cups of water in our oceans.

Is God *for* me? What type of question are we allowing ourselves to ask? It is to imagine that the God who made two hundred billion trillion stars—more stars than cups of water in our oceans—has regard for a single person. You. Me.

No person, it has been said, can ever rise above their view of God.[1] Who we worship, what we worship, is irrevocably tied to who we become. Our worship predicts our identity.

Is God *for* me? Few questions are of greater consequence because few problems are of greater concern than the one this question addresses. It is the problem of our collective lostness. We live in a world where we lose all we love—it is not a question of whether. We are lost in the unfinished chapters robbed by death. We are, each one, lost in the inevitable seasons of change and the unwelcome turns of fate. Often, we are lost in the unforeseen or disregarded consequences of willful actions. Is there a God who is *for* us in this? For us in the sense that this God who creates stars beyond human imagination could seek after *my* welfare? Could be concerned with *your* well-being?

Without a new vision of God there can be no new vision of hope. Our world will not change, but I know this: if God is always with the winner, if God is always for the stronger, if God always backs the better person, he cannot be a God who is for me. Can God be *for* me? For years I have been lost in this question.

A true vision of God may be costly, but we must embrace it. Our theological imagination is too narrow, but we can redeem it—if we dare. If Jesus endured his garden of Gethsemane for us, his grace must be more boundless than we could know. Stronger than death itself. Vaster than the Gethsemanes that surround us. Does God have regard for me? Yes. God is for me, because God is for the lost.

Of course, such a vision seems audacious and absurd. To believe that the Creator of the heavens is on the side of a sinner?

1. Tozer, *Knowledge of the Holy*, 4–5.

This seems impossible to comprehend given all we think we know. Indeed, we might think we lack the strength to imagine God in a such a way, but that's just it. The story of God is the story of *his* search for us. The entire question hinges on him, *on who he is*, and not on us and our experiences.

Have you ever lost something very meaningless but expended every effort in finding it? My five young daughters often lose their most precious belongings (read: pieces of worthless plastic jewelry or mangy over-loved stuffed animals). Many nights I have expended frantic searches to retrieve these items. And I never find them soon enough. Why do I waste my time on this? Because my child's heart is precious to me. Take heart in this. God, too, is searching. Under the couch cushions, through our messes.

In the very center of the Gospel of Luke, in chapter 15, are three parables. These form the heart of Luke's Gospel. It is the only time in the Bible—the only time that we know of in history—where Jesus told the same parable in three different ways. In the Hebrew Bible, repetition was used as a form of emphasis, as when the mysterious, angelic Seraphim continuously declare God to be "holy, holy, holy" (Isa 6:3). Holiness is the only attribute of God to be emphasized this way. We will discuss that attribute in chapter 1, but for now it is important to see that these parables, whatever their singular message may be, are uniquely emphasized in the Gospel of Luke and, if we are to take Luke's message seriously, are uniquely emphasized by Jesus himself. They are the "holy, holy, holy" of Luke's Gospel. These three parables—the parable of a shepherd who loses one sheep, of a woman who loses one coin, and of a father who loses two sons (yes, there are two!)—they are images of mental revolution.

That is, most simply, what a parable is. These are not merely earthly stories with heavenly meanings. These are pictures of theological subversion. Yes, on one level Jesus loved to talk about common things: sheep, coins, farmers, seeds, kings, servants, lenders, priests, grain mills, vineyards, and sons. The characters in Jesus' parables are rarely divine. And yet, these stories are holy through and through. The parables of Jesus are *"where religion becomes secular without loss.*"[2] This is an apt description of the whole life of Jesus.

C. H. Dodd writes that a parable is "a metaphor or simile drawn from nature or common life, arresting the hearer by its vividness or strangeness, and leaving the mind in sufficient doubt about its precise application to tease it into active thought."[3] In other words, they are a challenge to imagine. In our case, as we will see, to imagine that God is a seeker. But more, that God is a sacrificer. God is a seeker of *us*, but he is a sacrificer of *himself*. God searches for the lost of Luke 15, and, as I hope you will discover, he finds them in people like us.

What lies ahead? This study combines reflective and critical readings of this key chapter of Luke's Gospel. It aims to present the three parables of this biblical text in the Greco-Roman and Jewish context of first century Palestine. How would these parables have been received? What do we know of Jesus' intended audience? The book further sets these questions within the historical situation of Jesus' journey toward his own crucifixion as well as his identity in Luke's Gospel as the unique son of Israel's God. Divine sonship in antiquity was attained through conquest and success; it was, most relevantly, granted through the adoption into the family of a deified emperor. But Jesus' trajectory was downward. A crucified God. This study aims to read Luke 15 in its historical context and within this revolutionary understanding. To repeat, these parables are challenges to theological revolution. Every chapter of this book aims to bring this out, excavating the historically rich yet relevant details of the text, moving through the biblical passages consecutively from the beginning to the end of this book. The first few chapters will lay the groundwork by discussing Luke's vision of Jesus.

This study touches on a personal topic. It is about us and God. Few things are more personal than that. It is all the more important, then, to frame the context appropriately. We cannot

2. Wilder, *Early Christian Rhetoric*, 87. Quoted in Rindge, "Luke's Artistic Parables," 414.

3. Dodd, *Parables of the Kingdom*, 5.

tether our faith to a drifting ship. We owe it to ourselves to pursue concrete, historical realities. The question of who God is—and how Jesus is related to him—is central to the whole life of Jesus, and without this we are in great danger of underappreciating the parables of Luke 15.

I must make it clear at the outset that our study is not merely a commentary on this text; it is also a theological study. We are asking a question about what *God is like*. This question not only influences our reading of Luke 15, but our reading of this text, in turn, influences our theology. Once we appreciate this, we find that God, the Creator of innumerable stars, is not merely *for* us. *It is to his honor to be so.*

There is an irony in the title of this book. *For People Like Us.* The title indicates the inclusive breadth of individuals for whom Luke 15 is intended. In short, it is for anyone. Simply, it is for *people.* The irony is that we spend relatively little time teasing this out compared to the time spent discussing God, God's relationship to Jesus, and, in turn, the relationship of Jesus to the parables of Luke 15.

This is purposeful. God's search of you does not depend on who you are. There are no criteria to fulfill. It depends absolutely and unreservedly on who he is.

1

Holy and Tender

THE EARLY AFTERNOON OF January 10, 2009, would mark one of the most memorable experiences in the life of a young waitress. She worked at a local, family-owned restaurant in Washington, DC, named Ben's Chili Bowl, and as a man approached her counter to pay for his lunch, he had his hand outstretched with a twenty dollar bill. "Would you like some cash back?" she asked him. "Nah, we straight," he said.[1]

There was nothing more to the experience than this. The twenty dollars included a generous tip, but not extraordinarily so. The man was kind but nothing beyond what the occasion would dictate. What made the occasion so memorable was that this man would, within ten days, be inaugurated as the forty-fourth president of the United States. When president-elect Barack Obama treated this young woman with respect and spoke to her like any other person would, it was unremarkable but for the fact of *who he was*.

We will listen to a child differently than we listen to a spouse and to a spouse differently than to a figure of great authority. And this is essential to keep in mind when we read about something from the life of Jesus. Reading one of the four Gospels is not much different than stepping into a Ben's Chili Bowl for our work shift

1. The occasion is discussed briefly in Young, "Argument against Code Switching," 49.

1

on a Saturday afternoon. Everything about these biographies is typical *but for the one who speaks to us through them.*

It is easy to miss the holiness of the life of Jesus, but it greets the careful reader at every turn. Broadly speaking, the Jewish conception of God was that of an altogether holy being. "Holy" in its simplest form meant "other." God is *other.* When I speak of God as "holy" in this book, I do not mean merely morally good or even morally superior. I do not mean it in this everyday sense, in the sense in which our holiness (moral purity) can or should reflect God's holiness (Lev 20:7; 1 Pet 1:15–16). I am speaking of so much more, of that attribute of God that causes those persons who encounter this being, as the Hebrew Bible describes, to become psychologically undone (Isa 6:5, Job 42:5–6).

This notion, as Stephen Seamands expresses, "is not narrowly conceived or understood. It does not have a precise, exact meaning, but, depending upon its context, is closely linked with other divine attributes or characteristics."[2] This is seen most clearly in Isa 6:1–8, in which holiness is related to God's love, God's purity, God's power, God's glory, and primarily to God's unrivalled majesty, what we might call his "transcendence."[3] God is holy in the sense that he transcends—that he exists *beyond*—the great divide that separates created things from the Creator. Holiness is the awful untouchable mystery of absolute power, absolute sovereignty, absolute purity. We could ask, "who is more like God in his holiness—a man, an angel, or an ant?" But that question, according to Isaiah's conception, is nonsense. Holiness is not a matter of degree or distance. It is a matter of quality. None of these things are any *more* like God than the other, not intrinsically. "To affirm that God is holy, then, is to affirm that there is an 'infinite qualitative difference' between the creature and the Creator, the human and the divine . . . there is an absolute gulf fixed between them which cannot be crossed."[4]

Holiness separates. This, in great part, is the reason behind the Jewish purity laws, the temple boundaries, and the many

2. Seamands, "Inclusive Vision," 80.

3. Seamands, "Inclusive Vision," 80–85.

4. Seamands, "Inclusive Vision," 81; see also Sproul, *Holiness of God*, 15–46.

dietary prohibitions that Jesus shattered, but this is to get ahead of ourselves. The relevant point for us now is this: the truly unappreciated and outrageous component of the Gospels is that they are, while being on the surface mere biographies about Jesus, more appropriately read as recollections of those who witnessed, in history, when the "infinite other" passed through the divide into our world. They had witnessed the unimaginable.

Only one person in the Hebrew scripture, for example, could still the storm (Ps 107:29; Job 38:8–11). This is God's prerogative only. But in the Gospels it is *Jesus* who does this (Matt 8:23–27; Luke 8:22–25). Only one person in the Hebrew scripture forgives sins (Ps 51:4; 2 Sam 12:13), but in the Gospels it is Jesus who does this (Mark 2:7; Luke 5:21). The book of Job describes God as the one who walks on the water (Job 9:8; cf. Sir 24:4–5), but in the Gospels, it is Jesus who does this (Mark 6:45–56; Matt 14:22–36). In this context Jesus says, "Take courage! It is I. Don't be afraid" (Mark 6:50).[5] In this instance Jesus comforts his disciples with a possible reference, however veiled, to the name of God himself. Mark 6:50 woodenly translates into, "Take courage! *I am.* Don't be afraid" (emphasis mine). The "I am" is how God designates himself in his revelation to Moses at the burning bush (Exod 3:14).

All of this marks the mere introduction to the greater mystery. I have spent many years studying the Gospels, especially the Gospel of Luke, and I have studied them as historical texts. Historically speaking, there is nothing significantly different *in kind* between the biographies of Jesus (the Gospels of the New Testament) and the biographies of the Roman emperors that were penned by the greatest biographers of antiquity. As I have discussed in much detail elsewhere, the names, details, and historical features of Luke's text create a strong argument that Luke received these stories from eyewitnesses.[6] This argument is not merely what one would call "cumulative," like a rope made up of many strands. It is "corroborative." That is, every piece of evidence not merely

5. Unless otherwise indicated, Bible translations are NIV.

6. Van de Weghe, "Cerebral Scars of Shipwreck," 205–20; "Beloved Eyewitness," 351–57; *Historical Tell*; "Name Recall."

strengthens the overall case but often also corroborates—that is, strengthens—another piece of evidence at the same time. It is as if when adding another string or chord onto a rope, a piece of thread also gets tangled up with another chord to make it thicker. Let me give a very brief example before I get to my point.

The amount of personal names found in the Gospel of Luke and how these names are distributed throughout this text is only found in historical sources of antiquity that rely on eyewitness accounts. This is the conclusion to a very intricate argument I have made elsewhere, building on the work of Richard Bauckham; a relevant point is that an ancient historical writer would sometimes name his source(s) implicitly by highlighting that character within the text, and there are especially good reasons for thinking that some of the Gospel authors did this.[7]

In Luke 5:1–11, we have the story of Peter. Peter was likely one of the "eyewitnesses from the beginning" who, according to Luke's prologue (Luke 1:1–4), reported their accounts to Luke the Evangelist. This passage describes the circumstance under which Jesus called the earliest disciples, Peter, Andrew, James, and John, to leave their fishing nets behind and follow him. The Gospels of both Luke and Mark describe this event, but Luke's describes it with much greater detail.

Why is this significant? Its significance comes when we realize Luke almost certainly relied on the Gospel of Mark as a written source.[8] Luke, in fact, treats the Gospel of Mark with more reverence than the Jewish historian Josephus treated his Hebrew Bible.[9] That is, aside from making grammatical adjustments, Luke rarely changes Mark's text, sometimes even following Mark's Gospel verbatim when they contain the same accounts. Luke is *more* than faithful to the Gospel of Mark as a written source; he follows Mark religiously. But here, Luke adds details and even changes some details from Mark's text.

7. Van de Weghe, *Historical Tell*; Bauckham, *Eyewitnesses*.

8. Goodacre, *Synoptic Problem*, 56–83.

9. Downing, "Josephus' Antiquities," 33.

This is a clue that we are onto something. Mark describes the scene very tersely: Jesus walks along the Sea of Galilee, calls these men, and they suddenly and inexplicitly leave all behind (Mark 1:16–20). Yet Luke adds loads of details into his account: what Peter felt (Luke 5:9), said, (5:1, 8), and experienced (5:6). Luke describes how Jesus tells Peter, who had fished in vain all night, to cast his net into the water, and how Peter and his companions consequently caught so many fish in a single instance that their boats began to sink while pulling in their nets. All of this adds richness to the narrative. And then Luke changes the name of the body of water upon which they were fishing from the Sea of Galilee, as Mark calls it (Mark 1:16), to the Lake Gennesaret (Luke 5:1).

Throughout Luke's Gospel he consistently replaces Mark's title, the Sea of Galilee, with the title "Lake Gennesaret" or, simply, "the lake" (Luke 8:23, 26, 33). This is all the more interesting when we learn from Josephus that the locals did not call that body of water the "Sea of Galilee," as Mark calls it, but that they called it "Lake Gennesar,"[10] a variant of the name only found in Luke's Gospel. It is likely that the Sea of Galilee is, in fact, a theologically motivated designation, but, again, that would take us beyond our discussion.[11]

The crux is that we can see even in this brief account how Luke may have relied on an eyewitness, in this case Peter. We see it in a convergence of items: the focus on a named individual, the additional detail from the perspective of this person, and the additional and unusual historical changes that Luke makes to the Gospel of Mark that are then corroborated by outside texts. This, then, serves to corroborate the other argument I have made elsewhere, that named characters in the Gospels often served as living footnotes, so to speak. Luke focuses so much on Peter in this text as if to imply, "Peter told me this story! Go ask him about it." But, as I mentioned, that conclusion is part of a much deeper discussion.[12]

---

10. Josephus, *War*, 3.463.

11. For further discussion, see Szkredka, "Call of Simon," 173–89; Notley, "Sea of Galilee," 183–88.

12. Van de Weghe, *Historical Tell*; "Name Recall."

For us, it takes us back into the mystery of it all. Because this text in Luke's Gospel is not just about a man (Jesus) who calls a few fishermen to follow him. That is how it reads in Mark's Gospel. It is, in Luke's Gospel, a story about a man (Peter) who comes face to face with the otherness of God.

Luke 5:1–11 has what we might call four stages. The first stage introduces the encounter (5:1–7): when Peter witnesses Jesus provide a miraculous catch of fish. The second stage is the confession (5:8): when Peter falls down at the feet of Jesus in awe, calls him "Lord," and declares his own sinfulness. The third is the restoration (5:9–10): when Jesus comforts Peter. The fourth is the commissioning (5:10b–11): when Jesus calls Peter to leave all and become "a fisher of people" (5:10).[13]

In the Revised Common Lectionary, a book used by many denominations to determine their Sunday Scripture readings, this passage in Luke 5:1–11 is always read in parallel to another text from the Hebrew Bible, Isa 6:1–8.[14] The reason for this is obvious. Isaiah, too, is called in four stages: encounter (6:1–4), confession (6:5–6), restoration (6:7), and commission (6:8–10). The parallels are particularly strong but also disturbing because of their implications: that "Jesus stands on the divine side of reality."[15] Luke 5:1–11, after all, describes how Peter met Jesus on the edge of a Palestinian lake, but Isaiah 6:1–8 describes how Isaiah met the Lord of the universe in his temple! It is the very passage, in fact, that we discussed earlier, the one wherein God is described as "holy, holy, holy." Peter met "the other" no less than Isaiah did, albeit it on an unassuming Tuesday morning, or on some other ordinary day at work.

It is clear is that history and revelation are intercrossed in Luke's biography of Jesus. The connection between Jesus' person and his identification with Israel's God is so strong in the Gospels, in fact, that it introduces a yet further curiosity. I will discuss this more at the end of chapter 3, so I just remark on it here. The

---

13. Green, *Gospel of Luke*, 233, labels these stages: epiphany, reaction, reassurance, and commission.

14. Hays, "Netted," 311–16.

15. Gathercole, *Preexistent Son*, 75.

Gospel writers do not seem to place the emphasis of Jesus' biographies within his ministry of healing, forgiveness, and mastery over nature, although the implicit links between Jesus and Yahweh in these instances are replete, as we discussed earlier. The focus of Jesus' ministry in the Gospels is the cross, especially so in the Gospel of John. This is odd, especially since John has such a clear focus on Jesus' divinity.

What can account for this? I think the answer is shockingly simple. The Gospel writers take the divine otherness of Jesus for granted. It was, so to speak, the old news. The good news, the Gospel, was something much more profound. That Jesus' servant-hood and crucifixion tore open the veil of heaven. This is what his resurrection proved. The resurrection was the Father's stamp of approval on Jesus' claims and his ministry—the claim that God was, in him, becoming a servant to save the lost. The Gospels do not merely tell us something about Jesus, that he is God in some vital sense; they tell us something about God, that God is like Jesus in some vital sense—that is, in his ultimate slavery and tenderness.

This is clearly marked out in the trajectory of Luke's Gospel with regard to Peter.[16] Peter encounters Jesus' divinity at the *very moment* that Jesus calls him (5:8). And this revelation intensifies until Peter makes his confession of Jesus' Messiahship (9:20) and experiences Jesus' transfiguration (9:28–36). When Peter, James, and John see Jesus unveiled on the mountain, therefore, it is not Jesus' divinity that is newly revealed to them, but something else. The Father calls Jesus "my chosen son" (9:35).

This is another change Luke makes to Mark's text, but this time it is for theological reasons. In the Gospel of Mark, the Father calls Jesus, "my beloved son" (Mark 9:7). Why does Luke change the quotation from "my beloved son" to "my chosen son"? Because the quotation Luke provides makes the link with Isa 41:2, rather than merely with Ps 2:7, more explicit: "here is my servant, whom I uphold, my chosen one in whom I delight."

16. For Luke's Christology in relationship to his eyewitness sources, see van de Weghe, "Early Divine Christology."

Darrell Bock notes, "Luke's change here explains his understanding of the wording and seems to derive from Isa 42:1, with its reference to the Servant as God's chosen instrument."[17] It is as if the Father was saying to Peter: "Now that you know that Jesus is a divine king, it is time to define that divine kingship in terms of servanthood and self-giving love, in the seeking of the lost even unto death." And at this point in Luke's Gospel, Jesus begins his journey to Jerusalem, where he will die (9:31, 51).

Why is this important for us? It is essential because the parables of Luke 15 are placed at the very center, in the epitome, of this self-identifying journey of the divine Jesus to the cross. The stories of Jesus, remember, are *where the religious becomes secular without loss*. Recall that this was said about the parables of Jesus but that it could be said about his whole ministry. The crown of heaven and the cross of earth—these are two opposites that come together in Jesus. How can this be?

Jonathan Edwards is known for his famous sermon, "Sinners in the Hands of an Angry God." But a far better and less known sermon of his is titled "The Excellency of Christ." In this sermon he reflects on how certain characteristics and events come together in the person of Jesus that otherwise *might forever remain separated*. In Jesus, infinite deity and finite humanity unite. In that moment of the cross, in the greatest shame and mockery, God revealed his greatest faithfulness and glory. In Jesus' greatness he nevertheless descended to the lowest of people. In him, holiness and tenderness greet us in one.

The media reported on the waitress's encounter with Barack Obama with praise. Why? He did nothing great or even unusual. He gave a waitress a tip and spoke to her like an ordinary person. But we recognize, even in this Saturday afternoon encounter, that when the greats stoop down to touch the earth, it is good. Why do we think this? I do not know. Is it because we live in a Christianized society? The idea, of course, is thoroughly Christian. Or is it because we intuitively think this is good? Perhaps it is an echo of the divine within us. Regardless, if it is good for a president-elect

17. Bock, *Theology of Luke*, 165.

to greet a waitress, is it not good for God to stoop down and seek us in our lostness? If it is to God's glory to be good, it invites us to begin to believe that God can be *for* us.

2

God's Search for the Lost

IN CHAPTER 1, WE set our conversation in perspective by discussing some big picture items that broadly color the backdrop to Luke 15. We cannot separate the parables from the person who told them. Jesus is presented as someone who crossed the Creator/creature divide and, in the context of Luke's Gospel, revealed the servant-like grace of God. This is especially emphasized in Jesus' final journey to Jerusalem (Luke 9:51—19:44), of which Luke 15 marks the approximate center.

This chapter will be brief and will be our last prelude before discussing Luke 15 specifically. Our subtitle indicates that this book is about God's search for the lost. Is this a legitimate perspective of what God is doing here in the ministry of Jesus? Is it even legitimate to speak of God being a part of the parables that we are about to discuss?

Some have argued that Jesus' parables, especially the parables we will look at, are not about Jesus or God at all. The parable of a lost sheep, according to Ernest van Eck, is "a story about a shepherd (not God or Jesus) and a sheep (not a sinner) that gets lost."[1] Amy-Jill Levine sees no hint of Jesus' search for the outcasts in this parable:

---

1. Van Eck, *Parables of Jesus*, 120.

> If we hold in abeyance, at least for the moment, the rush to read repenting and forgiving into the parable, then it does something more profound than repeat well-known messages. It provokes us with simple exhortations. Recognize that the one you have lost may be right in your own household . . . Don't wait until you receive an apology; you may never get one. Don't wait until you can muster the ability to forgive; you may never find it . . . Instead, go have lunch. Go celebrate, and invite others to join you. If the repenting and the forgiving come later, so much the better.[2]

There are reasons to question these perspectives, especially if we take the context of these stories within Luke's Gospel seriously. We should also heed the caution of John Donahue: "The revelation of God in parable cannot be reduced to a series of theological platitudes or moral maxims. Here we touch on one of the major problems of preaching on the parables: the tendency to soften their shock by moralizing them, that is, turning *the good news into good advice*."[3]

The Gospel of Luke has the most parables of any Gospel (thirty-three), and approximately half are unique (sixteen). Luke obviously saw great value in the stories that Jesus told, and it is all too easy to pass over their theological implications, especially as they relate to Luke's theme of Jesus' outreach to the outcast. Clearly, Luke used these short stories by Jesus to adorn the biographical portrait of him. Let us take, for example, the parable of the good Samaritan (Luke 10:25–37).

This parable has little indication that it contains theological allegory, but does that mean it is devoid of theological implications? It is one of Jesus' most well-known parables, and I am sure you likely know it. But to refresh, it is about a man who is robbed on his way to Jericho from Jerusalem. The robbers leave the man for dead, and eventually a priest, a Levite, and a Samaritan pass him by. Only the Samaritan helps the man, even paying for his care

---

2. Levine, *Short Stories by Jesus*, 75.

3. Donahue, *Gospel in Parable*, 16–17; emphasis mine.

at his own expense. The term "Good Samaritan" of course derives from this story.

Many will know, too, why Jesus told this parable. Remember that it was around a discussion about the greatest commandments of the Hebrew Bible: to love the lord your God with all of your heart, soul, mind, and strength, and, secondly, to love your neighbor as yourself (Luke 10:27; cf. Lev 19:18). Jesus told the parable in response to a lawyer's question, "Who is my neighbor?" The lawyer clearly wanted to limit the term "neighbor" to minimize his responsibility and, likely, to justify the restricted scope under which he applied this principle in his daily life (10:29). Jesus then responded not merely by demonstrating what it looked like to be a neighbor, but he demonstrated it by making the hero of the story a Samaritan. This is certainly the type of person the Jewish lawyer would never consider a neighbor. The Jews and Samaritans were vehement enemies; the Samaritans rejected many of the key sacred Jewish texts, worshiped at their own temple, and held a different conception of Yahweh.

One thing is often neglected, however. The very question that begins this discussion between Jesus and the lawyer in Luke 10:25 was this: "Teacher, what must I do to inherit eternal life?" Do you see how radical this parable now is? Not only is the Samaritan the hero in the story, but he reflects the person *that meets the requirements for inheriting eternal life* in the story-world of Jesus. This is truly radical. Is Jesus redefining the boundaries of who has access to eternal life? Parables can be subversive in this way, and Jesus' radical focus on inclusion often goes hand-in-hand with implication for his authority or deity.

To build off the observations of chapter 1, this divine undercurrent is especially seen in the acts of tenderness throughout Jesus' ministry, especially during his journey to Jerusalem (Luke 9:51—19:44). Luke 17:11–17, for example, emphasizes Jesus' compassion for outsiders and again involves a Samaritan. Ten lepers are healed by Jesus. One is a Samaritan, and nine are Jews.

Jesus tells them to show themselves to the priest; lepers lived in exile from the community, and it was customary, as we discuss in the next chapter, to have a priest examine you before allowing you back into the community. This Samaritan leper, then, would not have shown himself to a Jewish priest and would have gone to his own temple on Mount Gerizim. He alone, however, returns to Jesus and falls to his face at Jesus' feet (Luke 17:16). This is the type of action that elicits rebuke in Luke's writings elsewhere (Acts 10:25–26):

> Peter entered the house, Cornelius met him and fell at his feet in reverence. But Peter made him get up. "Stand up," he said, "I am only a man myself."

But Jesus says no such thing; he does not rebuke this leper. In fact, Jesus makes a comment that might seem offensive to us. He says, "has no one returned to give praise to God except this foreigner?"

The word "foreigner" here in Luke 17:18 is not meant to offend. It is a Greek word that is nowhere found outside of Jewish literature. It occurs in one prominent place in Israel, at the temple gates on the large signs that forbid the gentile "foreigners" from entering the temple upon pain of death.[4] This leper is like a man who fell at the feet of a priest in the temple, and Jesus pronounced him clean: "rise and go, your faith has made you well" (Luke 17:19). Luke's use of vocabulary allows for ambiguity, and the verse could also be translated: "rise and go, your faith has *saved* you" (emphasis mine). The entire account is filled with grace and theological implication. Is Jesus the embodiment of God's temple? Are ethnic and religious boundaries removed in him?

Lastly, let us look at the famous story of Zacchaeus, which bears several resemblances to Luke 15 and can act as the gateway to our discussions on that section of Luke's text in the following chapters. It has three similarities to Luke 15: a focus on an outsider (a tax collector, Zacchaeus), a meal (with Zacchaeus), and a concern for the lost. The significance of Jesus' dining habits and the nature of tax collectors will be discussed in the next two chapters, but for now let us focus on a statement that Jesus makes in light of his dinner with Zacchaeus. Recall that Zacchaeus was a chief tax

---

4. Hamm, "What the Samaritan Leper Sees," 284–85.

collector who climbed up a sycamore-fig tree to see Jesus and was then invited to dine with him. This is how the account continues (Luke 19:7–10):

> All the people saw this and began to mutter, "He has gone to be the guest of a sinner." But Zacchaeus stood up and said to the Lord, "Look, Lord! Here and now I give half of my possessions to the poor, and if I have cheated anybody out of anything, I will pay back four times the amount." Jesus said to him, "Today salvation has come to this house, because this man, too, is a son of Abraham. For the Son of Man came to seek and to save the lost."

Luke 19:7 is almost identical in content to Luke 15:1–2: "Now the tax collectors and sinners were all gathering around to hear Jesus. But the Pharisees and the teachers of the law muttered, 'This man welcomes sinners and eats with them.'" Luke 19:10 is also pertinent: "For the Son of Man came to seek and to save the lost." This is part of a group of sayings from Jesus that take the form of "I have come" plus a purpose clause. These sayings include things such as "I have come to bring a fire to the earth" (Luke 12:49). Another example would be "Do you think I came to bring peace on earth? No, I tell you, but division" (Luke 12:51).

Sometimes the phrase is spoken in the third person, with the Son of Man as the subject. Such is the case in the account with Zacchaeus discussed above (19:10). In such instances, Jesus is clearly referring to himself, and the title emphasizes Jesus in his earthly role, his passion, and his future resurrection. Of course, the saying begs the question: "where did Jesus *come from*?" Since the scope of these claims encompass the entirety of Jesus ministry (Mark 1:38, Luke 4:43; Luke 19:10), what does he mean by this? Jesus clearly is not saying that he came from Galilee to Jerusalem, but that he came to earth (implied: from heaven).

When Jesus uses such phraseology, he speaks as the angels do when they come from the divine realm to deliver a message.[5] Since Jesus is clearly no angel, this comment has two ramifications. First, it is a cryptic claim to preexistence. Second, it is a

---

5. Gathercole, *Preexistent Son*, 113–76.

claim that views Jesus' search for the lost as *the reason for this life-consuming mission.*

This is significant. When the then president-elect Barack Obama reached out to that Ben's Chili Bowl waitress in kindness, it was a good mark of his presidency, but when he executed Osama Bin Laden, it was heralded as a *great* mark of his presidency. The former event is hardly known, while latter hardly unknown. What marks the difference? The difference is that in the latter occurrence, he acted well in *fulfilling the expectations of his role* as a president. This was part of his job description as commander-in-chief. A carpenter is most celebrated for the houses he builds, a doctor for the patients she saves, a prosecutor for the criminals she successfully convicts. These are the honors of life-consuming vocations, rewards for intense devotion and sacrifice. It is natural to have pride in one's lifework. This has implications for how we think of Jesus. It was not a dishonor for Jesus to save Zacchaeus. He did not reluctantly invite himself over to Zacchaeus's house to dine with him, but the opposite. Jesus sought him out. He saw it as *his life's work* to seek the lost. It is his honor to save a sinner, to rescue the lost and the broken. Is God *for* me? We might be tempted to answer, "perhaps, reluctantly." No. Is God *for* me? Completely and passionately. It is his honor. His life's work is at stake.

When we say that Jesus displays both the holiness and the tenderness of God, we are saying more than that both exist despite one another. It is, as we discussed at the end of our last chapter, that they exist together in a person. Take, for example, the crucifixion of Jesus. This demonstrates the tenderness of God only because Jesus is holy. It demonstrates the holiness of God only because it is seen as an action of divine self-sacrifice.

What we encounter in Jesus is a holy tenderness. This is like the tenderness of an intimate friendship between a father and a child. When the father bolts his doors or provides house rules, is it because he is not a tender father? No, he does such things to protect his child and that tender relationship.

Jesus, too, is fiery, passionate, full of zeal. He divides households and brings fire. He overturns tables and throws out the moneychangers. But he does this why? To make room for a lost one. What did Jesus say to those moneychangers in the temple courts? "My house shall be called a house of prayer" (Luke 19:46). This is direction quotation from Isaiah 56:7: "for my house will be called a house of prayer for all nations." That passage that Jesus quotes is about a time foreseen by Isaiah, a time when the foreigners and outcasts, the physically disabled, would serve at God's temple. Jesus saw Isaiah's vision as his life's calling.

We should resist reading the parables as stories for children. The more we understand their historical frames, the more we feel their earthy dust, the more we will see the tenderness of God. But, too, they will subvert our expectations and surprise us. They are holy stories. They remind us that God "is faithful but free."[6] He is faithful to what we know him to be, but he is free to invite us into a deeper experience that expands our vision of him. Such is the experience of any spouse or intimate friend.

Jesus came down to show us what God was like. It was not in a storm. It was not in a triumvirate in which he fed and groomed his enemies only to slaughter them for his glory (more on this in the next chapter). It was the parade of his naked grace. This picture is not diminished in the apocalyptic literature of the New Testament: Jesus is still described in the book of Revelation as both a lion and a lamb, but then, too, like a "lamb that was slain" (Rev 5:1–10).

Why have I chosen to write on the parables of Luke 15? It is certainly because these stories are more than stories about sheep, sons, and coins. It is because they form the core of Luke's message, the gospel in a nutshell. Charles Dickens is rumored to have called one of its parables in particular "the best short story ever written."

Yet I think these parables are still more than this. Luke 15 is written, like John's Gospel, "that you may believe that Jesus is the Messiah, the Son of God, and that by believing you may have life in his name" (John 20:31). Such belief, I have found, is more like the endurance of the marathon runner than the swift success of a sprinter. Even a notable theologian such as Gresham Machen

6. Bauckham, *God Crucified*, 72.

could say, "some of us have known the blankness of doubt, the deadly discouragement, the perplexity of indecision, the vacillation between 'faith diversified by doubt,' and 'doubt diversified by faith.'"[7] The difficulty of the journey, as the invitation into that faith journey itself, is ordinary.

It is as ordinary to struggle as it is ordinary to be loved by God. It is part of the everyday. The message of Jesus' grace is for *ordinary* sufferers and sinners. You may think that your sin is extraordinary. I doubt it. Whatever it may be, it is likely not worthy of that adjective. We are all, in the end, more like Hitler than we are like Jesus. Extraordinary is the one who calls us, who made more stars than cups of water that we could imagine scooping up with our hands. Nevertheless, he crossed the Creator/creature divide, and when he did, with whom did he eat at his table? With those believed to be *extraordinarily* lost.

7. Stonehouse, *J. Gresham Machen*, 432.

3

The Invitation

Now the tax collectors and sinners were all gathering around
to hear Jesus. But the Pharisees and the teachers of the law
muttered, "This man welcomes sinners and eats with them."
Then Jesus told them this parable . . .

—LUKE 15:1–3

"THIS MAN WELCOMES SINNERS and eats with them." As Luke sets
the stage for Jesus' recitation of the parables of the lost, what is
the significance of this introductory detail? Why do the Pharisees
grumble in response?

It is a fitting comment to consider as we begin to look at Luke
15, because it allows us to apply the findings of our last two chapters to a particular situation. As we discussed, Jesus was remem-
bered by eyewitnesses as one who crossed the Creator/creature
divide and to embody God's temple. He saw his divine mission in
terms of seeking the lost. But for this to be meaningful to a reader
of Luke's Gospel, she or he must be able to identify with the group
that Jesus sought.

At the outset, let me make one brief comment. The Gospel of
Luke is the gospel of possibility. We see this in Luke 1:34, in Mary's

response to the surprising news that she will bear a son: "How will this be?" We see it in the manner by which the parable of the lost sons, as we will see, is left open-ended. We see it in the very grammar of Luke's Gospel.

Ten times the characters in Luke's Gospel ask the question, "what shall I do?" Three of these are on the lips of characters in parables. Many instances refer to matters of how to live our lives and how to handle our possessions.[1] These are all in the subjunctive mood. This is the mood of possibility. Cynthia Jarvis writes:

> In language the indicative mood is for facts and absolutes; the subjunctive mood is for hope and possibility, for faith held together with astonishment . . . a mood that would seem to correspond to the kind of truth both revealed and hidden in the Incarnation, a mood that refuses brute inevitability and the despotism of the fact.[2]

What shall I do? And what does this have to do with me? This is a legitimate question to ask ourselves, as even the grammar of Luke's Gospel invites us to do.

Concerning our text, it has been argued that the Pharisees' outrage at Jesus' habit to eat with sinners and tax collectors was motivated by their concern for ritual cleanliness, but some scholars have pushed back against this.[3] Although it is true that sinners and tax collectors, due to the nature of their lifestyles or their associations with Gentiles, were liable to ritual impurity, it is simply very difficult to envision this constricting their ability to eat at someone's table. There were many things that could make a person ritually unclean—sexual activity, childbirth, proximity to death, etc.—but these activities did not lead to significant social isolation. On the other hand, the Pharisees' preoccupation with purity laws is hard to deny. For now, we will table the purity discussion, and when we take a closer look at Jesus' audience in the next chapter, we will revisit the issue in greater depth.

1. Rindge, "Luke's Artistic Parables," 413–14.

2. Jarvis, "Ministry in the Subjunctive," 445.

3. Blomberg, "Authenticity and Significance," 215–50; cf. Wassen, "Jesus' Table Fellowship," 137–57.

Regardless, Jesus' guests were rejected by certain elements of society because they were seen as living outside of the blessing and law of God. Understand that the Pharisees, too, desired their repentance. John Kilgallen makes the following observation:

> The Pharisees, too, sought the conversion of sinners. They share the goal of Jesus; it is a question, then, of means. The Pharisees would never have considered Jesus' approach to sinners. Why not? . . . It seems right to say that they, like many others, think that association with evil will inevitably make one evil. Moreover, what is the right way to bring a sinner to his senses? By fraternizing with him, and thus dulling in him criticism of his sinfulness, or segregation, which becomes a clear, silent statement of reproach by the community with the hope of embarrassment, or its like, and repentance?[4]

What better way to pierce the hearts of sinners than by shunning them? We banish the rebel son in the hope that his desperation will spurn his return. Such was the reasoning of the Pharisees.

But this was not the way of Jesus. In each of the parables we'll discuss, the lost item does nothing to better its chances of being found. Similarly, Jesus never appears to require purity or reform *before* fellowshipping with sinners. Some scholars claim that Jesus *never* required repentance for entry into the kingdom of God.[5]

This goes too far, and Jesus' teachings are full of calls to repentance, even of radical challenges toward self-abandonment. But it is not clear that even these were not meant to lead *to* discipleship. It is easy to recall the rich young ruler who could not part with his possessions (Mark 10:22), but it is also easy to forget that Jesus, in his radical challenge to him, looked at him and loved him (10:21). Jesus had notoriety for a reason. His notoriety for tenderness to sinners can be misunderstood to mean that Jesus preached a cheap grace. The point here is not to argue that it was or that it was not. That was not Jesus' response, was it? His response was not a detailed self-justification. His response was to tell a story

4. Kilgallen, "Was Jesus Right?", 592–93.
5. Sanders, "Jesus and the Sinners," 34–52.

of a shepherd, a woman, and a father. It was to focus on the joy of God over a sinner who repents rather than to focus on God's sorrow over one who did not (Luke 15:7, 10).

We too might find ourselves at this table. Do we have our act together? Perhaps not. Do failure and disappointment mark our path? Perhaps they do. Perhaps all that this means is that we have come to the right place.

The Approachable Messiah

When Jesus' disciples labeled him as the Messiah they were generally terming him as a king. But the concept of Messiah was also understood in priestly terms (Ps 110:1–4). Ancient Judaism combined both from the beginning. Both King David and King Saul, the first kings of Israel, for example, performed priestly functions.

Mark George makes the case that Saul from *his very anointing onward* is depicted as priestly.[6] His case is intriguing. First, he highlights how the prophet Samuel, the one to anoint Saul to the kingship, seats Saul at the head of the table (1 Sam 9:22) and gives him the leg or thigh of the sacrifice, which Samuel had set aside for him. This is the portion of the animal set aside for the priests, as highlighted in the Torah. Second, when Saul cuts up the oxen in 1 Sam 11:7, a specific term that designates the ritual cutting up of animals is used (Ex 29:17; Lev 1:6, 12; 8:20). 1 Samuel 11:6 highlights this as taking place when "the Spirit of God came upon him in power." George argues that this explains Saul's obsession with cultic ritual throughout his career.[7]

The point is that at the very inception of Israel's monarchy, the first king at his first meal at the first table was a priestly king. Jesus, too, was seen as a priestly king. This is more central to understanding Jesus' activity of eating with sinners than has previously been recognized, but we will flesh this out in the next chapter. For now, recall our discussion above, on Luke 17:11–19, for example.

6. George, "Yhwh's Own Heart," 452.

7. 1 Sam 13:12; 15:13, 14; 20:21, 26; cf. Lev 7:20–21.

Sinners came to be forgiven by Jesus. Lepers came to be cleansed by him.

This was the work of a priest. In the Old Testament, if you were rendered impure, either physically and morally, separated from all others and isolated by your life's conditions, the first person you went to was a priest. And he was the first person who examined you upon your return after your cleansing. The priest was the most approachable of men. The puritan preacher Charles Spurgeon remarks:

> The true priest was truly the brother of all the people. There was no man in the whole camp so brotherly as Aaron. So much were Aaron and the priests who succeeded him the first points of contact with men, on God's behalf, that when a leper had become too unclean for anybody else to draw near to him, the last man who touched him was the priest. The house might be leprous, but the priest went into it, and the man might be leprous, but he talked with him, and examined him . . . and if afterwards that diseased man was cured, the first person who touched him must be a priest. "Go, show thyself to the priest," was the command to every recovering leper.[8]

You can admire great monarchs, but you cannot approach them. This brings us back to our former comparison of the Gospels with the biographies of the renowned Roman Caesars. Both Plutarch (c. 46–120 CE) and Suetonius (c. 69–122 CE) were ancient historians that wrote about ancient heroes. Both wrote, of course, about Julius Caesar. Caesar once spared one of his enemies. His name was Vercingetorix. He was the son of a Gallic leader and became the king to unite the Gauls in their campaign to defend their homeland against Caesar's war campaigns. Vercingetorix was a great warrior who, nevertheless, after a decisive battle, willingly surrendered to Caesar in order to save the rest of his men. Caesar immediately imprisoned him and sent him back to Rome. It was the year 52 BCE. Then Caesar cared for this man. He clothed him, fed him, and kept him alive. Caesar did all of this

---

8. Spurgeon, "Approachableness of Jesus."

with the contributions of his benefactors. He did this every day, for six years. He waited.

One day it was time for Caesar's first Roman triumph, a celebratory parade through the streets of Rome. A triumph was the highest honor that a general could attain to. It could only be conducted with the approval of the Senate and the people. During this parade, the general wore a laurel and rode in a four-horse chariot. And this warrior would be paraded through the streets, much like how Jesus rode on his donkey into Jerusalem. He would march into and through Rome, being praised by all, and before him would be a parade of his conquests.

Vercingetorix, along with a myriad of other items of conquest, was in this procession. At the proper time, at the end of the procession, in the temple of Jupiter, Caesar took this man that he had kept, fed, and prepared, like a rabbit for a Christmas meal, and had him strangled in front of the crowds. All those years and all that mercy was only for a single purpose—to give Caesar as much glory as possible in his death. But not so with Jesus. When he rode that donkey into Jerusalem, he was the one to be kept and killed on display. When he was beaten, he did not resist. When he was insulted, he was silent. While his enemies killed him, he prayed for their forgiveness as he died in agony.

The whole ceremony of Roman crucifixion was meant to be a mockery of coronation.[9] Hence, the robe and the crown of thorns. Hence, the final exaltation on a stake or a cross. But Jesus, in his love, took that mockery and turned it into reality. He showed us that what it meant to be truly regal, what it meant to be God-like, was mostly seen in that moment. Joel Marcus writes:

> The mockery that has transformed kingship into a joke encounters a sharper mockery that unmasks it, so that the derision of kingship is itself derided and true royalty emerges through negation of the negation. For many early Christians, this reversal of a reversal, which turned

9. Marcus, "Crucifixion as Parodic Exaltation," 73–87.

penal mockery on its head, was probably the inner meaning of Jesus' crucifixion.[10]

When he identified with the most hopeless, vile, and miserable parts of humanity at his crucifixion, it was at that moment that the first person outside of his group of disciples, a Roman centurion, recognized that he had seen the face of God (Mark 15:39; Matt 27:54). This is what both Mark and Matthew's text record: "Surely this man was the Son of God!" Luke 23:47 records the centurion saying something else: "Surely this was a righteous man."

Luke's text is an allusion to Isaiah's prophecy about a future, suffering servant (Isaiah 53:11): "After he has suffered, he will see the light of life and be satisfied; by his knowledge my righteous servant will justify many, and he will bear their iniquities." We will further discuss Luke's interest in drawing this comparison in chapter 7. But how can Mark/Matthew and Luke associate both things—deity and servanthood—with the death of Jesus? By now the answer should be obvious. In the servanthood of Jesus is the truest face of God. It is worth emphasizing again that it is to the glory of Jesus to be approachable. It is to his glory to have you at his table. The sinners and tax collectors gathered around him, the Pharisees grumbled, and Jesus told them a set of stories.

10. Marcus, "Crucifixion as Parodic Exaltation," 87.

4

The Audience

THIS STUDY IS SHAPED conceptually like a funnel. We began wide by discussing the person of Jesus, how he is recollected in the Gospels, especially in Luke's Gospel, and then how his divine ministry is one of servanthood. We then placed Luke 15 within that journey towards Jesus' own death, during which his divine revelation increasingly became associated with his search for the outcasts. As we kept these items in our attention, we began to narrow the funnel towards its center, discussing the nature of Jesus' fellowship with sinners in Luke 15:1–3 and his notoriety of grace. What might this mean for us?

As we continue to ask this question, we cannot ignore or oversimplify the persons named as the implicit audience of these stories in Luke 15:1–3: the Pharisees and the teachers of the law on the one hand, and the tax collectors and the sinners on the other. These groups experienced a shared despair, and their stratification and cultural strife were not created in a vacuum. Then, as throughout other periods of societal conflict, inequity was tied to economic and political desperation.

For People Like Us

The Pharisees and the Teachers of the Law

The Pharisees and teachers of the law are those said to *mutter* at Jesus; a continual state of action is signified by this verb. Just as tax collectors are a subset of the broader group of sinners in Luke's Gospel, so the teachers of the law are best seen as a subset of the Pharisees. The NIV translation of "teachers of the law" is an interpretation of a word that could be applied to any scribe under any capacity, but the NIV translation committee was right to emphasize that, in this context, these scribes were experts in Jewish law. In that capacity, they would be more interested in the basis of Jesus' authority, while the Pharisees more broadly seem to emphasize issues concerning purity and Sabbath observance.[1] Naturally, there is both overlap and distinction between these two groups, but since the teachers of the law are nowhere treated as a single group outside of the New Testament, we will not treat them further here.[2]

The Pharisees were victims of political lostness. The Roman occupation was the ruin of their people's legacy of independence. In the four hundred years of God's silence in between the Testaments, they faced the apparent failure of God's promise. They lived in the shadow of the Maccabees, a family of pious rebels who overthrew their Greek occupiers out of zeal for God's law, whose lineage itself eventually become corrupt.[3] The children of the Pharisees, like those of most Jews in Palestine during the time of Jesus, were named after this initial family of holy warriors. Did the Pharisees hope for a similar political revolution? It is possible. They were more moderate than the Zealots, whose uprising resulted in the destruction of Jerusalem in 70 CE, for example, but they also acted as their co-conspirators.[4]

1. See the discussion by Saldarini, *Pharisees, Scribes, and Sadducees*, 144–73.

2. Saldarini, *Pharisees, Scribes, and Sadducees*, 3–4.

3. Yinger, *Pharisees*, 22–35.

4. Yinger, *Pharisees*, 56–57.

Compromisers, surprisingly, may be the best word to describe them, forever stuck in the balance of powers. Even the scribal Pharisees who worked as upper-class bureaucrats were dependent on the ruling or governing class for whom they worked.[5] Likewise, their political influence was tied to their popularity with the locals, so that they were forced to balance their loyalty to the governing class with their popularity amongst the common people. The Pharisees had a reputation for piety but also for compassion and leniency. Those in the more sectarian communities such as Qumran, for example, referred to them as the "seekers of smooth things."[6]

All of this, given Jesus' vehement strife with them, may seem surprising to us. We will get to that. For now, realize that they built hedges around the law to ensure their purity, that they abided by additional, extra-biblical principles of living, but that they also did this in love. Such religious practices were commonplace in Judaism. They believed it is what God wanted.[7]

Their religious pride and their interest in public influence, the natural consequences of their circumstance, often left the Pharisees at odds with the message of Jesus. It is simplistic to see the Pharisees as villains. They were clingers to beliefs that darkened their ability to receive Jesus' message. But we cannot see the situation as black and white. This nuance is captured in Luke's parable in Luke 15:11–32, the parable of the lost sons. The older son is representative of the Pharisees. In the parable, he is upset because his father kills the fatted calf to celebrate the return of his wayward younger brother. The Father, a representative of God, does not condemn the older son for this response, however: "'My son,' the father said, 'you are always with me, and everything I have is yours'" (Luke 15:31). God's heart, likewise, is not against these people. The harsh words of Jesus against them elsewhere in the Gospels may shock us (Matt 23:13–39). But confrontation is not rejection. We must remember that Pharisees were included in the

5. Saldarini, *Pharisees, Scribes, and Sadducees*, 41–42.

6. Yinger, *Pharisees*, 90–91.

7. Kilgallen, "Was Jesus Right," 590–91; Yinger, *Pharisees*, 229.

group of early Christians in the book of Acts (15:5). The parables of Luke 15 are directed against them but are also an invitation toward them. We will discuss this more in chapter 8.

Tax Collectors and Sinners

Tax collectors and sinners, too, make up Jesus' audience (Luke 15:1). The former had taken advantage of a zero-sum economy. In such a system it is believed that someone's gain is always at another's expense. Most people lived at or below subsistent levels: "Those who had no problems with sustenance were altogether at most 10%, whereas in continuous problems of sustenance were living some 90% of the population, more than two thirds of them in severe or extreme poverty."[8] Tax collectors, likewise, were men with families who lived in an honor/shame culture, and they had families to protect and to feed. In opposition to Pharisees and Zealots, these men blatantly collaborated with the enemy to survive.

Pictures emerge from the Second World War of certain women with their heads shaved. These were women living in liberated Nazi-occupied Europe. Their hair had been cut off by their communities as an act of shaming; it branded them as traitors, because they had collaborated with their German occupiers. Many of these women had slept with German soldiers.

Tax collectors, likewise, were the traitors of God's people. They were like those who had slept with the enemy. In light of this, it is no coincidence that in Matthew's Gospel both prostitutes and tax collectors are linked together in a single group (Matt 21:31).[9] Jesus ate with both types of people. Jesus welcomed them. This verb in Luke 15:1 for "welcomes" is used fourteen times in the New Testament. It describes the way people anticipate God's deliverance. It also describes how servants wait to welcome their master. But here Jesus waits for traitors and eats with them. This, according to the Pharisees, would make Jesus morally questionable by

8. Häkkinen, "Poverty," 3.
9. Gibson, "Hoi Telōnai," 429–33.

association but also, as discussed in the last chapter, as one who approved of, and perhaps even enabled, sinful behavior.

Luke 15:1 naturally couples the tax collectors with another subgroup. These hearers, the sinners, included both the very rich but also those who were part of a class without hope. Economically, they might be identified with those who "had been forced off the land because of population pressures or they did not fit into society. They tended to be landless and itinerant with no normal family life and a high death rate. Illegal activities on the fringe of society were their best prospect for a livelihood."[10] Upward mobility was extremely unusual in such cases and likely never entertained. They were the prostitutes, as just discussed, and those who, like tax collectors, sold their religious identity and dignity for survival.

They belonged to a group of others with whom Jesus ate and lived, Samaritans and lepers. People so riddled with diseases of body and theology that they literally lived apart. Women and men rerouted their travels to avoid them. Jesus ran to them. These outcasts were, as we have seen, the frequent heroes of Jesus' stories. And they, in return, were shown, through Jesus, a new picture of God.

The Line

We must not read these two sets of characters in Luke 15:1–2 as wooden stereotypes. They were a people lost in life. They were a people who lived in a world of disease and death. In the time of Jesus, two of every five children born into that world died before they reached the age of ten. Few made it to the age of sixty.[11] There were no ambulances, no antibiotics, no basic understandings of hygiene. They lived in a world without hope. A summer's fever or a wound's infection—this is all it might take to end a person's life. Disability meant certain destitution. In this world, there was no hope for a leper. In this religious environment, there was no

10. See the discussion by Saldarini, *Pharisees, Scribes, and Sadducees,* 35–49.

11. Reed, "Instability in Jesus' Galilee," 43–65.

salvation for a Samaritan. In this culture, there was no redemption for a tax collector. The sinner and the pharisee were both survivors lost in the historical movements that birthed them.

Of course, none of this negates the reality of exploitation within these people groups, especially from within the upper to the lower classes. Jesus called the Pharisees lovers of money (Luke 16:14), and he indicated that the laws of the scribes burdened the common people (Matt 23:4). The Gospels clearly indicate exploitation by tax collectors, for example (Luke 19:8). Sinners in Jesus' day included the rich and powerful who exploited the poor and righteous. No wonder Jesus himself was called a "glutton" for associating with them (Luke 7:34). At the same time, lower class sinners, with whom Jesus also associated, *really were* robbers, bandits, prostitutes, and petty criminals.

These are merely the realities of everyday life; the line between victim and oppressor is not always so easily drawn. It cuts through the heart of people themselves. There are bad fathers who are great employers. Bad children who are battlefield heroes.

Both the enemies of Jesus and the followers of Jesus came from every class of society. Among his followers were tax collectors, fishermen, wealthy women, political zealots, and Pharisees. His greatest betrayer, Judas, came from within his own group, and those who joined Judas in opposing Jesus included common people, Herodians, Roman soldiers, and religious elites.

Perhaps the greatest division between Jesus and the Pharisees was where the line between the holy and the profane was drawn. The very name, Pharisee, likely derives from the word "separate," and potentially underscores the Pharisees' dedication to holy living.[12] This conflict around holiness ties together what we have discussed so far and is able to shed light on the Pharisees' opposition to Jesus.

For the Pharisees, holiness was a vertical separation. It meant distance from fellow people and a separation of custom and sacred space between the holy and common. Their concern for purity, as briefly mentioned in the last chapter, likely influenced their

12. Yinger, *Pharisees*, 37–38.

disdain for Jesus' dining with sinners. This was not due to any general purity laws at the time, but with the Pharisees' perception of themselves.

They washed their bowls, cups, and hands before meals and appear to have applied purification standards which were typically designated only for food to be given up for priestly sacrifices. Behind this attitude lies the likelihood that they desired all Israel to live in a state of priestly ritual purity (Mark 7:4; Luke 11:38).[13] Religious purity was a central issue in Jesus' day, as excavations of purification baths and vessels throughout Palestine demonstrate. From the rabbinic laws that we can date to before 70 CE, 67 percent, that is, 229, concern table purity.[14]

How much of this we can apply to the Pharisees is under dispute. We simply do not know enough about their detailed practices. But two things seem clear. First, the Pharisees likely applied priestly purity laws to their own meals, and this resulted in separation from sinners in general, including from those who, beyond their moral impurity, showed a disregard for Jewish purity laws.[15] Impurity was contagious.

Second, Jesus also saw himself tied to the priesthood in some capacity, but for him the issue flowed in the opposite direction. Up to this point, we have only been able to touch on this issue, but Jesus' holiness was contagious. Rather than becoming impure by touching or associating with lepers, sinners, and people with bodily discharges (Luke 8:43–48), these people appeared to become pure *through their contact with Jesus.*

While holiness for the Pharisees was a vertical separation, holiness for Jesus was a horizontal distinction. He carried the authority of holiness within himself. He was "other" from every class of society, from every person who ever lived. Holiness was therefore as unattainable without him as it was attainable with him.

Rather than separation, it was gained in proximity to him. Kent Yinger writes:

13. Yinger, *Pharisees*, 160.
14. Neusner, *Pharisees*, 313.
15. Harrington, "In Ritual Purity," 42–54.

For a number of reasons—Jewish wisdom, observing *kashrut*, communicable impurity—Pharisees probably generally avoided too much or too close intercourse with non-Pharisees. Jesus seemed supremely indifferent to all this; he ate with tax collectors and sinners at their table and in their home! He seemed to view holiness, or rather his holiness and the holiness of the inbreaking divine rule, as more powerful. Instead of impurity, it was the purity of the kingdom of God that was contagious. Hanna Stettler calls this the "infectious nature of holiness . . . It is in [Jesus] himself, the holy one of God, that God's holiness has arrived which overcomes impurity."[16]

This odd idea is uniquely anchored in the priesthood of the Hebrew Bible. There is a single hint in Ezekiel that the garments of priests were believed to carry a contagious holiness (Ezek 44:19), for example, and this is elsewhere especially applied to the high priest (Lev 21:10–12; Num 16:41–50; cf. Wis 18:20–25).[17] Remember what the woman with the flow of blood tells herself as she reaches for Jesus? "If I just touch his clothes, I will be healed" (Mark 5:28). No wonder that Jesus at the inception of his ministry is called "the holy one of God" by the unclean spirit (Mark 1:24), a title that is, again, only attributed in the singular to Aaron the high priest (Ps 106:16; Num 16:7).[18]

When Jesus' disciples were plucking grain on the Sabbath, Jesus defended his actions by telling a story about King David. David entered the sanctuary on the Sabbath when his companions were hungry, and he fed them the consecrated bread. But this was only lawful for the priest to do (1 Sam 21; Mark 2:23–28). Why was it lawful for Jesus' companions to pluck grain on the Sabbath? Because they, too, were in the presence of a priestly king like David.

The ideas of a royal and priestly messiah are closely combined in the Davidic Psalm 110, especially verses 1–4:

16. Yinger, *Pharisees*, 163; Stettler, *Heiligung bei Paulus*, 164, Yinger's translation.

17. Fletcher-Louis, "Jesus as the High Priestly Messiah," 66–70.

18. Fletcher-Louis, "Jesus as the High Priestly Messiah," 63.

> The Lord says to my lord: "Sit at my right hand until I
> make your enemies a footstool for your feet." The Lord
> will extend your mighty scepter from Zion, saying, "Rule
> in the midst of your enemies!"... The Lord has sworn and
> will not change his mind: "You are a priest forever, in the
> order of Melchizedek."

This psalm is one of the most quoted Old Testament texts in the
New Testament. Jesus himself quotes from it at a crucial stage of
his ministry (Luke 20:42; cf. Ps 110:1). It is a key text that led him
to the cross. Recall Jesus' challenge:

> Why is it said that the Messiah is the son of David? David
> himself declares in the Book of Psalms: "The Lord said to
> my Lord: 'Sit at my right hand until I make your enemies
> a footstool for your feet.'" David calls him "Lord." How
> then can he be his son?

The implication of Jesus' retort is that the Messiah is the Lord in a
more timeless sense, predating David himself. According to Jesus,
the text pointed to his own preexistence.

This uniting of divinity, humanity, and priesthood was captured most clearly as the high priest ministered on behalf of his
people. Herein he represented God in his glory to the extent that
Josephus remarks that the high priest, in this particular office, is
called by "the most honored of revered names," Yahweh[19]. The
twelve tribes of Israel were engraved on the high priest's breast-
plate (Exod 28:8–21); he also represented his people before God.
But the high priest's layered robes represented more. Their layers
of gold and purple and blue, in their vegetative descriptions, were
widely interpreted to represent all the cosmos.[20]

What happened in the most holy place in the ancient Jewish temple was understood to be cosmic. Although the high priest
wore simple linen garments to offer the sacrifices on the Day of
Atonement, the decorated temple, as well as the most holy place,
were widely interpreted, again, to reflect this earthly and cosmic

19. Josephus, *War*, 4.163–64.

20. Fletcher-Louis, "Jesus as the High Priestly Messiah," 158–61; e.g., Josephus, *Ant.* 3.180, 183–87.

scope.[21] When we imagine that God, the God who created more stars than there are cups of water in our oceans, could seek a sinner, we are illustrating in an imaginative exercise what the most holy place in the Jewish religious system was believed to communicate. All of this, likewise, is wrapped up in the person of Jesus.

Rather than being determined by prior performance, by status or personal cleanliness, purity through Jesus was available to potentially anyone. Sacredness was subjunctive, it forever existed in Jesus as a hope to be grasped hold of, a possibility to be actualized. In him. The Pharisees' rejection of this lies at the heart of their opposition.

The Pharisees and the sinners, were they villains or victims? Yes to both. But that cannot be the most relevant question. The most relevant question is this. Is Jesus *for* them? Even for the Pharisees? This is what the parables of Luke 15 are meant to disclose.

21. Levinson, "Temple and the World," 284–85.

5

The Risk

Suppose one of you has a hundred sheep and loses one of them. Doesn't he leave the ninety-nine in the open country and go after the lost sheep until he finds it? And when he finds it, he joyfully puts it on his shoulders and goes home. Then he calls his friends and neighbors together and says, "Rejoice with me; I have found my lost sheep." I tell you that in the same way there will be more rejoicing in heaven over one sinner who repents than over ninety-nine righteous persons who do not need to repent.

Or suppose a woman has ten silver coins and loses one. Doesn't she light a lamp, sweep the house and search carefully until she finds it? And when she finds it, she calls her friends and neighbors together and says, "Rejoice with me; I have found my lost coin." In the same way, I tell you, there is rejoicing in the presence of the angels of God over one sinner who repents.

—LUKE 15:4–10

For People Like Us

JESUS SEEMED TO SPECIALIZE in seeking lost people. The Gospel of Luke and the book of Acts can be seen like an ever-widening circle of Jesus' search. It begins in Nazareth and moves on to Capernaum, then to Nain and Samaria, then to Jericho and Jerusalem, then to Antioch and Rome. But it is no mere geographic movement. It spirals downward and widens to redraw boundaries of inclusion. It begins with pious priests and teachers of the law and moves to fisherman and to centurions, to foreign widows and to lepers, to sinners and to Samaritans, and out to the very people who put Jesus to his death on a cross. The parables we are now ready to look at reflect the spirit of this widening circle of inclusion.[1] It is a search party to the least of the lost.

Although a very crude picture, we could imagine these parables as the background of a poster. At its top, it reads "wanted." At its bottom, it reads "a lost one." In between is a picture of the sea of humanity. These parables dare us to begin to imagine that God is *for* us.

Two unexpected characters greet us as Jesus gives his first two parables. Both characters are poor. Both characters are desperate. Both characters are irresponsible.

The reason this may be unclear to us is because we have been taught to misread these stories for centuries. Often we equate this story with other stories about good shepherds or metaphors of God as a good shepherd. These metaphors spring from the nomadic cultures of the Old Testament when shepherds had a good reputation. During the time of Jesus, his audience lived in an agrarian society with limited goods. Land was precious, and those who trespassed upon it uninvited were enemies.[2]

This is but one of several reasons why Jesus' contemporaries viewed shepherds on par with tax collectors. Shepherding was among the lowest-paid professions in the time of Jesus. Both shepherd and sheep "are bewildered creatures of low status, if not overtly despised then at least marginalized and ignored—with shepherding considered a vile and religiously forbidden profession

---

1. See Eng's discussion, "Widening Circle," 1–9.
2. For a fuller discussion, see van Eck, "In the Kingdom," 1–10.

in Jesus' day."[3] A shepherd, if he worked year-round, had just enough food to provide for his family. But a shepherd was rarely home to watch over his own family—yet another reason why his job was considered with disdain.

Shepherds roamed the countryside and carried weapons for self-protection. Their poverty, isolation, nomadic existence, and their likelihood of being armed led many to turn to banditry to make ends meet. They were a lost people. Jeremias writes, "the shepherd and sheep in Jesus' parable appear to share a similar lot and unenviable plight. Both are bewildered creatures of low status, if not overtly despised then at least marginalized and ignored—with shepherding considered a vile and religiously forbidden profession in Jesus' day." This interpretation of how the shepherd was meant to be viewed in this parable is generally in line with what we see in much of the Gospels and the parables of Jesus, the heroes of which are often the marginalized and outcast, whether they be tax collectors, prostitutes, lepers, or Samaritans.

Commentators grapple with the problem presented here by Jesus. This irresponsible shepherd leaves the ninety-nine. He leaves them. Alone. It has been suggested that the shepherd had a helper, that these sheep were his own possessions, and that this owner likely left the ninety-nine with this servant.[4] But it was very unusual for a shepherd to own his own flock; he took care of his flock on behalf of an owner who spent his time on activities that justified the owner's time, and a shepherd typically took care of a flock alone. A size of a hundred sheep was the normal size.[5] Why would this shepherd, then, leave the ninety-nine?

Jesus rushes to tell a second parable. This time the hero is a *heroine*. She is, likewise, poor. We will see why in a moment. But she is also foolish. She had lost one of ten drachmas. Ten drachmas could provide a poor household with food for approximately two weeks. The house would have been a small stone enclosure with few windows and little natural light. It was possible to lose small

---

3. Dykstra, "Finding Ourselves Lost," 742.

4. Van Eck, "In the Kingdom," 4.

5. Cf. the discussion by Wendland, "Finding Some Lost Aspects," 37.

items in-between the cracks of the stone floor. We do not know if she had a husband or lived alone, only that she has lost a vital possession. She, too, does something unexpected which is easily missed. She lights a lamp. During the time of Jesus, oil for lighting lamps was a valuable resource. It would cost the woman approximately the same value as the lost coin if she searched too long.[6]

The parables are both parables about risk. Unexpected actors take unexpected risks. What drives them to do this? Desperation. The shepherd, too, was responsible for the flock under his care. His monthly wages amounted to approximately sixteen drachmas. As mentioned, this is just enough to provide food for a small family, but nothing else. If he lost his sheep due to negligence, he was responsible to pay the full amount. A female sheep could cost him up to twenty drachmas while a male sheep was close to ten.[7]

We now have an insight into what is happening in these parables. This shepherd and this woman act out of desperation. Why risk the ninety-nine? It is a matter of survival. Why waste precious oil to search for a single coin? Because you need it desperately. No wonder Jesus says that she searched "diligently."[8]

Both the shepherd and the woman wager. They wager that the possibility of gaining back what was lost was worth the risk of losing even more. No wonder they both rejoice! Hope had danced on a razor's edge.

God, Jesus implies, is like this shepherd and this woman, and heaven rejoices when God's risk pays off. Ernest van Eck makes the point well:

> Finally, being part of the kingdom is risky, some would even say irresponsible. Telling stories like this parable—stories that cut against the social and religious grain of the day; stories that challenge the normalcies of society; stories in direct opposition to the way "we do things here"; stories that shock and question the status quo, power,

6. Vearncombe, "Papyrological Backgrounds," 8–10; van Eck, "Gaining or Losing," 1–9.

7. Van Eck, *Parables of Jesus*, 132.

8. Van Eck, "Gaining or Losing," 7.

and privilege; and stories that characteristically call for a reversal of roles and so frustrate common expectations are risky. Some people would say that telling stories of a different world, of the way things ought to be, of "life as ruled by God's generosity and goodness"—stories that re-envision the actual world in wholly unaccustomed ways and offer its hearers an alternative world to the world created by aristocratic society (Rome), by privilege and power, by tradition and custom, by religious authorities, by temple rituals and sacred texts—is irresponsible. Such a storyteller can, after all, end up on a cross.[9]

The risk in Jesus' ministry, in his actions and in his rhetoric, is clear. But what do these parables tell us about God? What is God risking in the ministry of Jesus? In the context of Luke 15:1–2, the risk is clear: "He welcomes sinners and eats with them!" The reputation of Jesus was at stake. And, given his authority among the people and all that we have discussed in the preceding chapters, so was the reputation of God. Holiness. Purity. Otherness. Jesus was running a great risk indeed. One might end up believing that God belongs where Jesus was clearly headed. On a cross. But crosses were common things. It is reported that the Romans crucified so many Jews during the siege of Jerusalem that they ran out of room to place their crosses outside of its city walls.[10] Through the eyes of antiquity, crucifixions are taboo, are offensive, are unspeakably awful—but they are not special. The cross is taken for granted.

And this is indeed what has happened. Christianity, more than any other religion, is the old sweatshirt in the closet. Worn in and faded. Loved well and stretched out. Easy to take for granted. The most comfortable of all. This is the risk of the shepherd God. A renegade of grace. Irresponsible in his pursuit. Is it pursuit warranted by the many? No, it is warranted by one. One lost one. Old sweatshirts, after many mud streaks and cold rains, fit us well, and are cast aside. But if God, the God who made the stars and oceans, risked becoming like that so that he might find us, how can he not

---

9. Van Eck, *Parables of Jesus*, 139.

10. See Josephus, *War*, 5.451.

For People Like Us

be *for* us? A grown sheep is a seventy-pound animal. If it gets lost, it dies. Sheep are extremely senseless animals. But the shepherd bears it upon his shoulders and carries it home. When he arrives home, heaven rejoices. The risk paid off.

Kenneth Bailey, who spent his adult life in the Middle East, saw in this parable a glimpse of the atonement; that is, he saw a picture in this story of God's sacrificial love. He appreciated the rugged terrain in which this shepherd would have found himself. He reflected on the weight of carrying such a large animal up and down the hillsides of Galilee. When he surveyed the artwork depicting this parable through the ages, he noticed a progression; while modern depictions increasingly paint the sheep as a mere lamb, a twenty- or thirty-pound animal, the earliest frescos show a shepherd carrying a large, adult sheep.[11] It was a picture of God's strength and sacrifice.

Given the discussions of our preceding chapters, Joel Green's remarks seem on point: "this parable is fundamentally about God, [its] aim is to lay bare the nature of the divine response to the recovery of the lost."[12] God's response is joy: "Rejoice with me; I have found my lost sheep" (Luke 15:6). As we discussed in chapter 2, this is not merely the type of joy one has over the recovery of a lost item. It is not *less* than that surely. But it surely more than that. It is the joy of a doctor who put it all on the line to save a dying patient with an unusually intricate or unorthodox procedure. It is the joy of a prosecutor who coaxed the confession from the murderer as a last-ditch attempt to achieve justice. God's joy over a sinner who repents is the joy that makes the sacrifice worthwhile. All the trampling of holiness, all the commonness of Christianity—in Jesus, God has scars and sweat and a cross. Yet in Jesus God saves sinners. And heaven rejoices.

This brings me to a final point. In these parables, the rawness and authenticity of history and the glory of divine revelation are especially seen. "Heaven" or "the angels of heaven" are

11. Bailey, *Cross and the Prodigal*, 31–32.

12. Green, *Gospel of Luke*, 574; quoted in Dykstra, "Finding Ourselves Lost," 741.

circumlocutions for God in these parables. This exchange of "God" for something akin to "heaven" is a way that pious Jews would avoid referring to God directly. This was an act of reverence. Luke does not do this elsewhere, but Matthew does it frequently in his Gospel, exchanging Mark's "kingdom of God" with the phrase "kingdom of heaven," for example. Why does Luke include this circumlocution here and nowhere else? This is may be an indicator that Luke is being faithful to an earlier tradition in this case, and that this early interpretation of Jesus' parables by Jesus himself goes back to an early setting.

It further demonstrates that the association of these parables with the character of God is not an editorial afterthought from Luke the Evangelist and may be intrinsic to the way that these parables were meant to be understood from the beginning. Concerning the divine implications of these parables, Frank Stagg observes:

> The reference to God is emphatic in the concluding application to two of these parables. That about a man and his sheep concludes with the application, "Just so, I tell you, there will be more joy in heaven over one sinner who repents than over ninety-nine righteous persons who need no repentance (15:7). The parable of the woman and her coin concludes: "Just so, I tell you, there is joy before the angels of God over one sinner who repents" (15:10). That God is not spoken of more directly is due to the piety that so revered the name of God as to hesitate to call it directly. The application is not explicit in the parable of the father and two sons, but it follows logically.[13]

Thus far, we see the "holy, holy, holy" of Luke's Gospel, the parables in Luke 15, deepening our vision of what God is like. This vision reflects both the subversive theology of Jesus, the upside-down nature of his challenge to imagine, but also his gracious call, his priestly invitation, to see ourselves as those who sit at his table.

---

13. Stagg, "Luke's Theological Use," 226.

6

Madness That Knows No Bounds

Jesus continued: "There was a man who had two sons. The younger one said to his father, 'Father, give me my share of the estate.' So he divided his property between them. Not long after that, the younger son got together all he had, set off for a distant country and there squandered his wealth in wild living."

—LUKE 15:11–13

ONCE JESUS IS FINISHED with his stories of a lost sheep and a lost coin, he begins to share what has been called "the greatest short story of all time." This parable is referred to in Shakespeare's *The Merchant of Venice* and has inspired masterpieces such as Charles Dickens's *Great Expectations*, engravings such as Albrecht Dürer's *The Prodigal Amongst the Pigs*, paintings such as Rembrandt's *Return of the Prodigal Son*, and lyrics amongst artists as diverse as Everlast, The Killers, Keith Green, the Rolling Stones, and U2.

Elements of the parable have entered our common language. Even Michael Scott from *The Office*, when reuniting with Jim, could say, "the prod . . . er . . . progidal . . . uh . . . my son returns,"[1] with the assumption that his audience would understand the reference, however fumbled it was. This is quite a revealing moment. It demonstrates that for many, the traditional title of this parable is still familiar to them *without even knowing what the title means.* This is reflective of the parable's tremendous impact over the ages.

"There was a man who had two sons" (Luke 15:11). The hero in this story is no reckless shepherd, no solitary woman, but a respectable owner of an estate with servants and fatted calves to spare. Jesus tells us that this father, however, is the most foolish of all. It is not his money that makes him foolish. It is not a lack of status. It is the love for a son.

There is something timeless about this son. With the world before him, he gathers his portion of the father's wealth. And he runs. There is some discussion over the legitimacy of the son's request. Some claim that the son's request for his inheritance amounts to him wishing his father dead, but this goes too far; nevertheless, it doubtless was a shocking and audacious request.[2] More audacious is the father's response. The father acquiesces rather than rebukes. Moreso, the father gives over his property (lit. "his life") between them. The father gives it all.

The parable indicates that both the father and the son act dishonorably here. The father apparently ignores the wisdom of the ancient scribe, Ben Sira: "In all that you do retain control . . . When the days of your life reach their end, at the time of your death distribute your property" (Sir 33.23–24 NRSV). Likewise, land and possessions in Jewish antiquity were highly prized and controlled by family bonds. This is reflected in the biblical legislations for marriage and land distribution, which were crafted to ensure that land remained tied to a particular family line into perpetuity to the greatest extent possible. In this instance, the younger son sells off not merely what his father would have worked for, but likely

1. *The Office.* 2006. Season 3, episode 2, "The Convention." Directed by Ken Whittingham. Aired Sep 28, 2006 on NBC.

2. E.g., Scott, "Heroes from on High," 142; see the discussion by Levine, *Short Stories by Jesus,* 51–52.

what his father was given by the generations preceding him. The younger son's share would have been less than a third of the estate, given inheritance regulations and the fact that a double portion was granted to the firstborn son.[3]

The father's permissiveness extends beyond granting the wish of dividing the inheritance prematurely. In such a case, the father retains the right as the ultimate executor of the possessions until his death, which explains some of the events that follow (specifically, that the father still wields authority over the estate, see Luke 15:22–23).[4] At any instance, the father *could* have regained control over his son's actions and prevented him from selling off the family possessions. No such actions appear to have been taken. Daniel Eng comments, "The parable does not indicate that the father had any sense of propriety in acquiescing to his son. While societal expectations dictated that he punishes his son to uphold the family honour, he does not. The father thus adds to the family's shame."[5]

The son, in response, takes all his father's grace—all that his father worked for and gave to him—and he wastes it with what has been understood and translated as "wild living," "a prodigal lifestyle," or what Walter Bauer refers to as "a madness that knows no bounds."[6] This is where the term "prodigal" comes from. "Prodigal" means "lavish" or "wasteful." Trevor Burke argues that "the parable of the prodigal son" is an inappropriate title; it is better titled, for reasons we will see, "the parable of the prodigal father."[7]

> After he had spent everything, there was a severe famine in that whole country, and he began to be in need. So he went and hired himself out to a citizen of that country, who sent him to his fields to feed pigs. He longed to fill his stomach with the pods that the pigs were eating, but no one gave him anything. (Luke 15:14–16)

3. Snodgrass, *Stories with Intent*, 131–33.
4. Snodgrass, *Stories with Intent*, 132; Eng, "Widening Circle," 3.
5. Eng, "Widening Circle," 4.
6. Bauer, *A Greek-English Lexicon*, 148.
7. Burke, "Prodigal Father," 217–38.

The details of the younger's son condition resonate with the timeless, common afflictions that have faced every generation: failure, desperation, and abandonment. Although the older son would later tell his father that the younger son "wasted his inheritance on prostitutes," it is unclear if Jesus intends us to believe this. There is nothing in the parable, per se, that indicates that this younger son's exploits were sexual in nature versus a mere reckless opportunism. The point is that he gambled it all. And lost.

Following his complete failure, the son was exposed to the types of famine that ravished Palestine and its surrounding regions on a regular basis. Just as the death rates in antiquity peaked in the summer months due to lack of clean water and the increase of seasonal disease, famines likewise were commonly so crippling that the gods of the Middle East were often those specifically tied to providing rain and storm. Everything hinged on the seasonal harvest. Like many, the younger son was both a responsible agent and unwitting victim in his circumstance. He was forced to sell himself to foreigner, to "a citizen," who, under such a contract, had complete authority over the man's daily life.[8]

In this case, it was the son's task to feed this foreigner's pigs. All of this was emphasized by Jesus to paint of a picture of this man as a reckless, foolish failure. Pigs were so loathed by Jewish people that archeologists use the presence or absence of their bones to determine the settlement distributions of Jews in antiquity. In their eyes, they were the most unclean of animals, and this younger son was not even permitted, so to speak, to eat the food that fell from the pigs' table (cf. Matt 15:27). Klyne Snodgrass emphasizes this point:

> Taking care of swine was viewed with disdain even in the Greco-Roman world, but Jews were prohibited from raising swine at all since the OT labels them as unclean, to be neither eaten nor touched. The Mishnah states explicitly "None may rear swine anywhere" (m. Baba Qamma 7.7), to which the Talmud adds "Cursed be the man who would breed swine and cursed be the man who

8. Harrill, "Indentured Labor," 714–17.

would teach his son Grecian Wisdom" (b. Baba Qamma 82b). The analogy between the prodigal who joined himself to a Gentile to feed pigs and tax collectors who joined themselves to the Romans is obvious.[9]

The son was in a worse condition than the dogs that roamed the streets of Palestine. He was like a harlot who sold herself for survival. He was a tax collector who betrayed his people. He was like a leper, unclean and exiled and hopeless. He was, in other words, like all the people that moved Jesus.

> When he came to his senses, he said, "How many of my father's hired servants have food to spare, and here I am starving to death! I will set out and go back to my father and say to him: Father, I have sinned against heaven and against you. I am no longer worthy to be called your son; make me like one of your hired servants." So he got up and went to his father. (Luke 15:17–20)

Everything we have learned about first-century Jewish culture increases the shame that runs through the story. It is shameful for a son to demand his father's inheritance before he dies. It is shameful to abandon your family. It is shameful to neglect to care for your father in his old age. It is shameful to squander your inheritance and your family's name. It is shameful to abandon your identity as a Sabbath-observant Jew, which the younger son surely would have done under his new labor contract. It is shameful to feed the pigs of a foreigner.

At this moment, the son literally "comes to himself." Although some Bible teachers claim that this amounts to his repentance, there are several reasons to doubt it.[10] The internal dialogue reveals that the son comes to his senses only so far as to devise a plan to escape his poverty. The phrase merely indicates that the son "came to his senses."[11]

9. Snodgrass, *Stories with Intent*, 126.

10. E.g., MacArthur, *Prodigal Son*; Young, *Parables*, 146.

11. Hultgren, *Parables of Jesus*, 76.

Whenever there is internal dialogue in the parables in Luke's Gospel, they give the hearer or reader insight into the depravity of a character's intentions. For example, the rich hoarder says to himself, "This is what I'll do. I will tear down my barns and build bigger ones . . . And I'll say to myself, 'You have plenty of grain laid up for many years. Take life easy; eat, drink and be merry'" (Luke 12:18–19). The shrewd manager, before unjustly reducing the debts of his master's debtors, says, "What shall I do now? My master is taking away my job. I'm not strong enough to dig, and I'm ashamed to beg . . ." (Luke 16:3). Every instance of internal dialogue in a parable of Luke's Gospel seems designed to accentuate moral ambiguity.[12]

Moreso, the younger son rehearses his lines: "I have sinned against heaven and against you," and these words mirror those of Pharoah to Moses: "I have sinned against God and against you" (Exod 10:16).[13] This son's heart is no softer than the Egyptian. But he believes his father has food to spare. So he leaves (likely under the cover of darkness), abandoning the obligations of his labor contract, and decides to become his father's servant instead.

> But while he was still a long way off, his father saw him and was filled with compassion for him; he ran to his son, threw his arms around him and kissed him. The son said to him, "Father, I have sinned against heaven and against you. I am no longer worthy to be called your son."
> But the father said to his servants, "Quick! Bring the best robe and put it on him. Put a ring on his finger and sandals on his feet. Bring the fattened calf and kill it. Let's have a feast and celebrate." (Luke 15:20b–23)

This son had lost it all. He is a man who has compromised all his ideals only to wind up alone and without prospect. This man is a waste of a life.

But when his father sees him, his shame, too, knows no bounds. Seeing his child from a far distance, he runs with self-abandon to embrace him. This father, too, has been shameful. He

12. Sellew, "Interior Monologue," 239–53.
13. Bailey, *Finding the Lost*, 131.

failed to discipline his son. He failed to keep him from wrongdo-
ing. And now he fails to be honorable. Grown men in Palestine
are not encouraged to hike up their robes to run, exposing their
legs.[14] But the father does so much more. He gives a dishonorable
son the "best robe." Whose robe is this? The father's own. He gives
his son the signet ring of responsibility. Whose ring is this? The
father's own. And he slaughters the fatted calf for him. Such a calf
could feed up to a hundred people; the whole village would likely
be invited.[15]

There would be a great party. But it would also be a completely unexpected party, and this creates an insight into the father's
joy. A fatted calf took approximately six months to prepare for a
slaughter after its birth. It would be penned up and confined to
limit weight loss. These animals were not merely there for the taking at any moment, but they were groomed for special occasions
such as weddings or communal feasts.[16] The father must already
have been grooming this calf for a special occasion. Its slaughter
did not merely result in an extravagant feast for a wasteful son, it
meant that whatever occasion the father had saved it for would be
deprived of its fatted calf. This is why the father is the true "prodigal." He is prodigal, wasteful, excessive, in his gracious joy. His is a
madness that knows no bounds.

Everyone at this party would know. They would know that
this father is reckless. He is a foolish father. The entire parable is so
outrageous that some scholars have argued, indeed, that the telling
of it must have been comedic. Jesus told a joke. But the joke, it
appears, is on those who think they understand what God is like.[17]
In this parable, the father runs *to him who may have no intention
of repenting*. The sheep cannot rescue itself. The coin cannot find
itself. This son cannot save himself.

---

14. Snodgrass, *Stories with Intent*, 126.
15. Casey, "Parable of God's Love," 36.
16. Macarthur, "Extraordinary Celebration."
17. Doole, "Observational Comedy," 181–210.

This is where God has found us. Think about this: this is where God finds *me*. When I have lost my hope in him, God has not lost his hope in me. Trevor Burke notes:

> In God's economy the hearer is confronted with what could otherwise be described as the scandalous arithmetic of divine grace. God is prepared to love lavishly, extravagantly, wastefully—a prodigal love for a prodigal people. In short, this is love cast wide without limits, "*a God whose love surpasses all typical expressions known to humanity.*"[18]

Some of those listening to the parable so far would see themselves in this father. As upper-level bureaucrats and administrators, it might be hard to identify with a poor shepherd or a poor woman. But the boundless love for a child is timeless and cross-cultural, and, as Amy-Jill Levine comments, "Jewish fathers of the first century were not, at least according to the sources we have (which should be the sources that inform our history), distant or wrathful."[19]

If a father becomes extravagant in his love for a son, should God, so the story implies, not be extravagant in his love for a sinner? Maybe. That depends. It depends on the person who tells the story.

We could imagine this parable being told in a modern context. Imagine stepping into Ben's Chili Bowl in Washington, DC, on that Saturday afternoon. But now instead of president-elect Barack Obama, a homeless, itinerant preacher is sitting at a table. Surrounding him are prostitutes and drug addicts, pedophiles, and felons, but also lawyers and plumbers and secretaries and members of Al Qaeda—people of all kinds. Across the table from him is Billy Graham Jr. or Beth Moore or Charles Swindoll. Imagine any one of these renowned Bible teachers.

The homeless man and the Bible teacher are discussing grace. Now imagine that this homeless preacher tells a story about a father and his son, implying that God's offer of forgiveness extends

---

18. Burke, "Prodigal Father," 237; Hultgren, *Parable of Jesus*, 86 (emphasis added by Burke).

19. Levine, *Short Stories by Jesus*, 61.

to those without prospect, to those riddled with heretical theology, corruption, and shame. But Charles Swindoll disagrees.

Millions tune in to hear Pastor Swindoll on a weekly basis. This homeless preacher has an eclectic, ragtag following of disenchanted outcasts. Who are you more likely to believe? Not only does the itinerant seem less reliable than the Bible teacher, but his claim seems more outrageous.

There are two things I must point out at this juncture. The first is the importance of all that we have said about Jesus in our earlier chapters. His embodied "otherness." His high-priestly, contagious purity. His role as a divine seeker. Without these things, the parables of Luke 15 are only the ramblings of a homeless evangelist.

And that brings me to the second point. *That is what Jesus was.* Jesus was a penniless traveler. Jesus, when he told the greatest short story ever told, had already set his eyes on the slave's death of the cross. These parables become both believable and meaningful *only when we appreciate where Jesus has come from and where Jesus is going.* We have spent significant time discussing where Jesus has come from—his claims and his divine actions—and in our next chapter, before we finish reading this parable, we will take a brief pause to appreciate where Jesus is going.

7

Most Like Jesus

"For this son of mine was dead and is alive again; he was lost and is found."

—LUKE 15:24a

WHAT DRIVES THE FATHER in the parable to run to his son and give him the best of everything? Jesus tells us that it is his compassion (v. 20). "Filled with compassion." This is how Jesus describes the father. The Greek verb here paints a vivid, strange image for us. In our modern world, we speak as if we feel things with our hearts. In Jesus' world, they felt with their bowels. Literarily, the father's bowels churned within him. He felt this emotion within his guts. And he ran. This verb translated as "filled with compassion" only appears three times in the Gospel of Luke. It is never used by the Roman biographers when describing the Caesars. It paints too vulnerable a picture. Once, Jesus is said to "feel it in his bowels"—to have compassion—on a woman whose son had died. On another occasion the hero of another parable, the Good Samaritan, feels compassion for a man left half-dead on the side of the street. And in this parable, the father is filled with compassion for his child.

For People Like Us

These three occasions share two characteristics. First, every time Luke records the verb it takes place at the exact middle of his story. To be more precise, the verb occurs in the literary midpoint. It is always the central verb in the narrative. This is so remarkable that some have argued that Luke *intentionally designed this to be the case.*[1] Regardless, it is always the turning point. Second, every time Luke records the verb it is felt in the presence of death, whether physical or metaphorical. A dead son is brought back to life. How? By the compassion of Jesus. A half-dead man is saved. How? The compassion of a Samaritan (an unlikely hero). A son is received back from the far country. How? The compassion of a father. Recall the father's words, repeated twice: "For this son of mine was dead and is alive again; he was lost and is found" (Luke 15:24, 32).

The parable, of course, is not just a story about a father, is it? Recall what is happening in the background of this parable. First, as discussed briefly in chapter 1, Jesus is on a trip to Jerusalem. We will get back to that. Second, Jesus tells this parable in response to accusations *against his character.* The parable is about more than men. It is about God's compassion for sinners. But at the same time, it is about Jesus.

This parable is about a new way to see God as father. But even on this revolutionary level, on the level of a God running for the unrepentant, the parable falls short of what the Christian story is about. When you think of it, who in the parable is Jesus *really* the most like? This is a very different question from asking, "which character is meant to represent Jesus in the parable?" That is not the question we are asking. When we reflect on this parable, *if* we had to liken the life of Jesus to any one person in this parable, whose role would we choose for him?

The story of Jesus is one in which he leaves his place of comfort, His Father's house. He is the one who travels to the far country: here, with us. He is rejected and abandoned, hungry and indentured. He is the one who dies. He is the one who is alive again. The one who wears the crown of the Father *is Jesus.*

1. Menken, "Position of σπλαγχνίζεσθαι," 107–14.

This is how early commentators such as Origin once read this parable, and it was a typical interpretation up until the time of Adolf Jülicher, a German New Testament scholar who in the late nineteenth century turned the tide away from allegorical interpretations of the parables. Nevertheless, even the famous theologian Karl Barth draws the connection between Jesus and the prodigal son; he sees Jesus' incarnation and resurrection forever hovering in its background:

> In the going out and coming in of the lost son in his relationship with the father we have a most illuminating parallel to the way trodden by Jesus Christ in the work of atonement, to His humiliation and exaltation. Or better, the going out and coming in of the lost son, and therefore the fall and blessing of [the human], takes place on the horizon of the humiliation and exaltation of Jesus Christ and therefore of the atonement made in Him. It has this as its higher law. It is illuminated by it.[2]

It is not my intention to argue that this is an accurate reading of the parable *as it was intended to be understood.* Nevertheless, when one begins to look at the parable through the lens of Jesus' overall ministry, an image of the ministry of Jesus does emerge from within the parable.

Remember that Luke 15 is situated amid Jesus' journey to Jerusalem. It is Jesus' trip to his *exodus,* as Luke calls it (Luke 9:31); that is, it is Jesus' trip to his death in Jerusalem. This is repeated many times (Luke 9:22, 44; 18:31; see also, 22:44)—Luke leaves us with no doubt: we know, and Jesus knows, where he is going. The far country.

Jesus is depicted in terms of the suffering servant of Isa-53—the one who is "pierced for our transgression" (Isa 53:5) and the one whose "punishment that brought us peace was on him, and by his wounds we are healed" (Isa 53:5). This connection between Jesus and the suffering servant is increasingly highlighted in the Gospel of Luke, especially in Jesus' death in which, as Vincent

2. Quoted by Cox, "Parable of God," 222.

Taylor remarks, Luke depicts Jesus as the servant of the Lord without using the name."[3]

Sometimes a parable fails to capture the deepest of truths
such as this. Jesus took the lot of the younger son, but *only because
he takes our place.* The cross that lay before Jesus, that end that increasingly consumed his imagination and distress, was the slave's
death. That is what it was called. In Latin, *servile supplicium.*[4] This
was a death we know little of because the Roman writers refused
to speak of it. It was "the most wretched of deaths."[5] It was ultimate torture. It happened naked. It was designed to extend agony.
Mark Finney remarks, "the victim's disgrace was compounded by
his nakedness, his bodily defecation, and the fact that wild beasts
(wolves, bears, lions) or birds may have attacked the victim at vital
parts of the body."[6]

Yet in the cross of Jesus, as in the parable of the lost son, we
are meant to see a picture of God. Although mentioned in passing
throughout our initial chapters, I did not do justice in highlighting
the scandal of it. Historian and author Tom Holland, in writing
about the views of ancient Greeks and Romans, writes this:

> Divinity, then, was for the very greatest of the great: for
> victors, and heroes, and kings. Its measure was the power
> to torture one's enemies, not to suffer it oneself: to nail
> them to the rocks of a mountain, or to turn them into
> spiders, or to blind and crucify them after conquering
> the world. That a man who had himself been crucified
> might be hailed as a god could not help but be seen by
> people everywhere across the Roman world as scandal-
> ous, obscene, grotesque.[7]

For the Jewish people, the cross was seen as a curse. It was the
curse of God (Deut 21:23): "Cursed is everyone who hangs on a

3. Taylor, *Passion Narrative*, 13; see also, Van de Weghe, "Early Divine
Christology."

4. Finney, "Crucifixion," 125.

5. Josephus, *War* 7.6.4.

6. Finney, "Crucifixion," 127.

7. Holland, *Dominion*, 6.

tree." To the Jews, then, Jesus' death was not merely a loss of life, but it was a loss of the favor of God the Father. Tom Holland goes on:

> The Jews, unlike their rulers, did not believe that a man might become a god; they believed that there was only the one almighty, eternal deity. Creator of the heavens and the earth, he was worshipped by them as the Most High God, the Lord of Hosts, the Master of all the Earth. Empires were his to order; mountains to melt like wax. That such a god, of all gods, might have had a son, and that this son, suffering the fate of a slave, might have been tortured to death on a cross, were claims as stupefying as they were, to most Jews, repellent. No more shocking a reversal of their most devoutly held assumptions could possibly have been imagined. Not merely blasphemy, it was madness.[8]

Madness. Yet beauty. This is what the earliest Christians saw in the death of Jesus. Long within their Jewish traditions had they carried shadows to a light not yet seen. There was the story of Isaac, the sacrifice of an only son, and his rescue through substitution (Gen 22:1–19). The story of the Passover, the deliverance of an enslaved people through the protection of an innocent, slain creature (Ex 12:1–13). There was, on their Day of Atonement, the transfer of their sin to the scapegoat and the goat bound for slaughter (Lev 16). Then, finally, in Isa 53, the sacrifice of a mysterious servant on behalf of the many.

For ages, these had been stories of awe and brutality. The temple was soaked in the blood of innocence. Substitution, in their eyes, meant purity. It meant holiness. But it was cloaked in the violence of slaughter. Then, in the death of Jesus, they came to see and to believe something about a man. That this man, Jesus, embodied God's holiness. And that all along, in their obscure and blood-filled legacy, they had foreshadowed the self-giving sacrifice of God's son. "By his wounds we are healed" (Is 53:5). This reality—the crucifixion of the holy—continues to inspire a kaleidoscope of reflection.

8. Holland, *Dominion*, 6.

For People Like Us

How can it be? Why? What precisely did it accomplish? But the early Christians lived anew in the "*that*" of the crucifixion. As they have through the ages. We live in the reality, as Paul did, that Jesus "loved me and gave himself for me" (Gal 2:20).

> What, then, shall we say in response to these things? If God is for us, who can be against us? He who did not spare his own Son, but gave him up for us all—how will he not also, along with him, graciously give us all things? (Rom 8:31–32)

The story of Jesus is much more subversive than the parable alone indicates. It is not about a father who gives all to his son. It is about a father who gives his son *for all*. It is about a son who became like a slave to set others free. In the death of Jesus he became our substitute. He enters our story. He carries our alienation and our guilt. He joins us in the far country.

There is little hope for a lost son, but absolutely no hope for a man on a cross. But out of that utterly hopeless, foul death God raised his son. Why? Hope and proof. It means that there is hope for what we may yet face; it means there is proof of who God now is. He is waiting for our return.

This is the fact that became the consuming obsession of the apostle Paul, the author of the passage from Romans quoted just above. Paul was once himself a persecutor. Paul was once zealous about opposing the message of Jesus. Had he been there, he would have stood in this crowd of listeners. Listening to and rejecting the words of these parables. He was, like the audience, after all, a Pharisee. Yet, as we will see, this last parable in particular was meant especially for them.

8

Counter

"Meanwhile, the older son was in the field. When he came near the house, he heard music and dancing. So he called one of the servants and asked him what was going on. 'Your brother has come,' he replied, 'and your father has killed the fattened calf because he has him back safe and sound.'

"The older brother became angry and refused to go in. So his father went out and pleaded with him. But he answered his father, 'Look! All these years I've been slaving for you and never disobeyed your orders. Yet you never gave me even a young goat so I could celebrate with my friends. But when this son of yours who has squandered your property with prostitutes comes home, you kill the fattened calf for him!'

"'My son,' the father said, 'you are always with me, and everything I have is yours. But we had to celebrate and be glad, because this brother of yours was dead and is alive again; he was lost and is found.'"

—LUKE 15:25-31

For People Like Us

WE ALL LIVE WITHIN the stories we tell ourselves. It has been said that "he who tells the stories rules the world." We are, among all creatures, the only one we know of that tells and lives in stories.

Much has changed since the days in which Jesus told the final portion of this last parable. Today, there are no gladiator games or crucifixions, no temples or animal sacrifices. But much like the time of Jesus, we are surrounded by story. Lifelong commitments become love stories. Accruals of wealth become rags-to-riches testimonies. The wars of our fathers are replayed in the dramas of unsung heroes. The power of media is in the broadest sense but a testimony to the power of story.[1]

"Myth" is a term scholars use to classify the grandest stories we have ever told. There are modern and ancient myths. These often center around a trope, a key concept, an unspoken notion recognizable to the audience. The Princess Bride has the damsel in distress. The modern detective drama has the apathetic hero, the reluctant good guy with a checkered past. One of the oldest tropes is seen in the savior-myth like that found in the story of Luke Skywalker. It involves an obscure beginning, an adventure or a journey, a point of testing and darkness, and then a resurrection of hope and a victory. The story of Jesus, too, is such a story. Of course, in the case of Jesus, the story, the myth, became true.

Judaism, too, carried several tropes within its sacred traditions. One was perhaps the most common of all. It was, really, a tale as old as time. It was the story of Cain and Abel. The older, rejected brother kills the younger, favored son, and the older brother is banished. The pattern repeats in Abraham's story when Ishmael is his firstborn son; but Isaac, the younger, is nevertheless the chosen. Ishmael, too, is banished. And again, Jacob, the younger scoundrel, is blessed, while Esau, the older, more responsible worker is cursed. "Esau I hated but Jacob I loved" (Mal. 1:2). Here is a saying from the rabbis:

> God has set the love of little children in their father's
> hearts. For example, there was a king who had two sons,
> one grown up, the other a little one. The grown-up one

1. See the discussion by Scott, "Heroes from on High," 135–44.

was scrubbed clean, and the little one was covered with dirt, but the king loved the little one more than he loved the grown-up one.[2]

Western history, too, has been influenced by this trope. Almost without exception, every painting, every homily, and even every title of this parable has been focused on one lost son, on the prodigal son. It is the younger son's parable, is it not? It is read at the expense of the older son. The truth is much more subversive. Amy-Jill Levine writes:

As all biblically literate people know, the beginning words of this parable, "There was a man who had two sons," introduce a literary convention. As these readers also know, we do well to identify with the younger son. However, the story in Luke 15 is a parable, and parables usually do not do what we might expect.[3]

Consider several striking features of Luke 15. First, the pattern in the three parables is broken by the older son. The first parable is about a lost sheep; the sheep is found, and the neighbors rejoice. The second parable is about a lost coin; the coin is found, and the neighbors rejoice. The third parable is about a lost son; the son is found, and the neighbors rejoice. There is reason to think that all of these parables are really just one parable, told in three different ways.[4] But if this is the case, if this pattern reflects the purpose of the parable(s), surely this entire ordeal with the older brother is not necessary to the story. It is narrative extravagance. Why, then, is there anything about the old brother to begin with?

Consider a second, simple pattern across the parable(s). The first part of Luke 15 is a story about something lost *away* from home (the sheep); the second part is about something lost *at* home (the coin). The next part is about something lost away from home (the younger son). The last part should be, then, about something

<hr>

2. Braude, *Midrash on the Psalms*, 1:131; quoted by Scott, "Heroes from on High," 142.

3. Levine, *Short Stories by Jesus*, 50.

4. Blajer, "Narrative Study," 129–30.

lost *at* home. This is what the older son represents. He is the prodigal who stayed with dad. And in the first century honor-shame
culture of Palestine, the older son's behavior is just a reprehensible
as that of the younger son.[5]

The older son, whose job it would have been to host the feast,
refuses to join in (Luke 15:28). Worse, when his father shames
himself further by running out to the older son, likely within ear-
shot of a community of guests (a fatted calf, after all, fed a community of people), the older son denies his father and slanders his
younger brother (Luke 15:29–30). Every first century hearer would
anticipate the older brother's punishment. Even more, they might
anticipate his banishment and rejection. This is a familiar story.
The stories of Cain, Ishmael, and Esau are playing out in him.

But the ending is possibly the most surprising element of all.
The father calls the older son *teknon*. This is the most endearing
term available and means not merely "my son," but "my child."
And with this gentle word comes a promise. His father's house will
be his forever (Luke 15:31).

The parable contains both invitation and revolution. First, it
is in invitation to those who would later turn and kill Jesus. The
old brother is certainly a reflection of Jesus' interlocutors, the
Pharisees and the scribes, while the younger son represents the
sinners and tax collectors. Second, the parable is nothing less than
the revolution of an old paradigm. It is a counter-myth.

Even today it is a continually held belief that the proverbial
"older" must be rejected for the "younger." The villain must die for
the hero. The enemy must lose so that we might win. Jesus offers
a different view of God. Concerning Luke 15:11–31 as a whole,
Bernard Brandon Scott writes:

> The father does not behave like a god punishing the
> wicked and unjust. He is a fool. "You want my property
> before I die? Take it. You want to come back? Here, come
> back, let's have a party. You don't want to come in to the
> party? I'll come out. You feel abandoned and unwanted?
> You're always with me." Whatever the children want he

5. Eng, "Widening Circle," 6.

gives them. Most significantly, in the parable the forgiveness of the younger son is neither achieved nor vindicated at the expense of the elder's rejection.[6]

This is a kind of grace that exceeds all others. It is for good reason
that this parable has had such an influence on the world, although
I doubt that the world has appreciated its true depth.

Often, we find ourselves in the place of the young son. Lost
in the squandering. Alone in despair. Ready to face the turning
point. But how much more often do we find ourselves at the mill,
in the grind of disappointed obedience. Our joys are lost in the
bitterness. Our kisses become cold obligations. *Is this all there is?*
We are like those who die the slow death. No sudden heartbreak.
No unanticipated disaster. Just a slow, earthy, and disappointing
loss of glory.

Is God still *for* us? This parable would dare us to believe that
he is. That the older son is loved. He is a tenderly loved child. His
father will always be with him. What a promise! Paradigm shifts,
too, need not happen in sudden transformations. They can be the
change of mind after long years of quiet struggles. The subtle, unappreciated ending of a story can be the most extravagant of all.

Klyn Snodgrass, in his learned commentary on the parables,
expresses this about the parable of the lost sons:

> No parable provides as much material for theological
> reflection as this one. Its use of metaphors and ideas for
> distance is instructive. The prodigal does not belong in
> the far country and in the alliance he has made. He is
> distant from himself, but both he and his brother are
> distant from their father in different ways. Most of us
> also live fractured lives, knowing neither unity within
> ourselves nor the familial relationship with God that has
> been offered to us. The specter of death haunts the par-
> able as well. The parable's message is that both sinners
> and seemingly righteous people—both the irreligious
> and the religious—have a home with God. They belong
> at home in God's family. The parable is more than theo-
> logical ideas about God's character; it is an invitation to

6. Scott, "Heroes from on High," 143.

recognize our estrangement and bankruptcy. For good reason Rembrandt's painting of the prodigal in Dresden's Zwinger Gemäldegalerie is a self-portrait of Rembrandt with his girlfriend Saskia. The prodigals are not the other people. At the same time, the parable is an invitation to return to our true selves—to come to ourselves (v. 17), return to God, and be willing to be embraced by God.[7]

7. Snodgrass, *Stories with Intent*, 141.

9

Joy

"I tell you that in the same way there will be more rejoicing in heaven over one sinner who repents than over ninety-nine righteous persons who do not need to repent."

—LUKE 15:7

"In the same way, I tell you, there is rejoicing in the presence of the angels of God over one sinner who repents."

—LUKE 15:10

"But we had to celebrate and be glad, because this brother of yours was dead and is alive again; he was lost and is found."

—LUKE 15:32

IN THIS FINAL CHAPTER, we will reflect briefly on the theme of joy in the Gospel of Luke. This theme is pervasive in Luke 15, as Frank Stagg notes: "Celebration as proper to the recovery of the lost is at the heart of these parables. The joy at the recovery of a lost sheep, a lost coin, or a lost son demands that joy be shared and

celebrated."[1] This joy, as Stagg goes on to emphasize, is linked
with the emphasis on God as a seeker and finder: "in effect, Jesus
is saying to his religious critics that God is like a man who recovers
his lost sheep; God is like a woman who recovers her lost coin;
God is like a father who recovers one lost son and strives to recover
the other lost son."[2]

Our study has linked together several themes: the divine dis-
closure of Jesus, the revelation of God in the cross of Jesus, and the
revelation of God in these parables of Jesus. The combination of
these features, we have argued, demonstrates not merely that it is a
part of Jesus' divine activity to be a seeker of the lost, but that it is
to his glory and honor to do so.

Joy and Honor

We see this highlighted in what the celebrations in the parables
are truly about. The first two celebrations—that of the found sheep
and the found coin—are rather comedic. It seems overblown to
throw a party for a sheep and a coin, after all, but that is not the
point. The joy for the shepherd was what the found sheep meant
to him. It meant that his honor was restored and that his wager
paid off. It reflected his dedication and his strength. To take the
risk and to hoist this animal upon his shoulders in haste to find his
flock complete—there was a story here to tell. Who was its hero?
Naturally, it was the shepherd himself.[3]

The coin, likewise, is hardly an object worth calling one's
neighbors and friends over! But there would have been a story
here. A reflection on the frantic searching and on the woman's own
diligence. Again, this woman's honor as a safekeeper of her family's
income has been upheld, and that is cause for rejoicing. It was not,
ultimately, about the coin; it was about honor.

1. Stagg, "Luke's Theological Use," 226.
2. Stagg, "Luke's Theological Use," 226.
3. Bailey, *Good Shepherd*, 201–3.

Ironically, the final parable is not so different. It is also fundamentally about risk. Not the son's risk, which did not pay off. But it is about the father's risk. The foolishness of the father, as we have discussed, is apparent from the beginning. One can imagine the talk of the town. "This man will never get his son back—he should have disciplined him from the outset." "Why did this father give this child such freedom?" "This man is full of weakness." "He condones the sin of his child by his permissiveness." It is no coincidence that the Pharisees grumbled for the same reasons about Jesus. No sinner will repent when you invite him to your table, will they?

And then the son's return changed it all. When the father threw that party, it was not a mere celebration of his son's free and full return. It was a justification of the father's own actions in the parable. Let them say what they will say. The father's vindication was in the celebrated presence of his long-lost son.

Joy and Reversal

Joy and divine vindication come together in other portions of Luke's Gospel as well. When God's upside-down plan is doubted, when Jesus' radically gracious ministry is questioned, the final justification of this ministry will amount to celebration. Towards the end of John the Baptist's life, as he lay in wait for his own death in Herod Antipas' prison, he doubted the ministry of Jesus. Likely John had anticipated the kind of Messiah who would kill God's enemies and restore God's honor in a display of power. During this time, Luke records that Jesus heals both a centurion's servant and a widow's son from Nain (Luke 7:1–10; 7:11–17). In other words, as John the Baptist was confined in shackles, Jesus was out healing the servants of Romans and sons of foreigners. John sent emissaries to Jesus to ask if he was really the Messiah after all.

> When his messengers came to Jesus, they said, "John the Baptist sent us to you to ask, 'Are you the one who is to come, or should we expect someone else?'"

> At that very time Jesus cured many who had dis-
> eases, sicknesses and evil spirits, and gave sight to many
> who were blind. So he replied to the messengers, "Go
> back and report to John what you have seen and heard:
> The blind receive sight, the lame walk, those who have
> leprosy are cleansed, the deaf hear, the dead are raised,
> and the good news is proclaimed to the poor. Blessed is
> anyone who does not stumble on account of me." (Luke
> 7:20–23)

Jesus responded to John the Baptist with a quotation from
the Book of Isaiah, which largely reflected Jesus' ministry to the
outcasts of society (cf. Luke 4:18–19; Is 61:1–2). This ministry to
the outcasts and to foreigners is what from the beginning of Jesus'
ministry had led those of his hometown to drive him up to the
edge of Nazareth to kill him (Luke 4:28–30), and his increasingly
blatant advocacy on behalf of the lost, with his increasing hostility
to those in power, were what led to his inevitable death in Jerusalem.[4] This mission encompasses his whole life. Jesus says to John:
"Blessed is anyone who does not stumble on account of me" (Luke
7:23). We no longer use the word "blessed" in a colloquial sense,
but in the context it simple means "happy."

"Those who accept this fact about my ministry," Jesus is saying, "will end up being happy because they will end up being vindicated." The sheep will be found. The son will return home. And
the party will celebrate that the Messiah was a seeker, and that it
was good. Luke goes on to narrate a cryptic set of sayings from
Jesus (Luke 7:24–35):

> After John's messengers left, Jesus began to speak to the
> crowd about John: "What did you go out into the wilder-
> ness to see? A reed swayed by the wind? If not, what did
> you go out to see? A man dressed in fine clothes? No,
> those who wear expensive clothes and indulge in luxury
> are in palaces. But what did you go out to see? A prophet?
> Yes, I tell you, and more than a prophet. This is the one
> about whom it is written: 'I will send my messenger
> ahead of you, who will prepare your way before you.'

4. See Van de Weghe, *Historical Tell.*

I tell you, among those born of women there is no one greater than John; yet the one who is least in the kingdom of God is greater than he." (All the people, even the tax collectors, when they heard Jesus' words, acknowledged that God's way was right, because they had been baptized by John. But the Pharisees and the experts in the law rejected God's purpose for themselves, because they had not been baptized by John.)

Jesus went on to say, "To what, then, can I compare the people of this generation? What are they like? They are like children sitting in the marketplace and calling out to each other: 'We played the pipe for you, and you did not dance; we sang a dirge, and you did not cry.' For John the Baptist came neither eating bread nor drinking wine, and you say, 'He has a demon.' The Son of Man came eating and drinking, and you say, 'Here is a glutton and a drunkard, a friend of tax collectors and sinners.' But wisdom is proved right by all her children."

This is a lengthy, difficult section of Luke's text, but it reflects exactly what we have just discussed. When Jesus refers to "a reed in swayed by the wind" and "a man dressed in purple," it is almost certainly a covert reference to Herod Antipas, whose inscription on coins was accompanied by a swaying reed (this is because Jews refused to allow the images of rulers on coins, per the second commandment).[5] Likewise, purple was the color of royalty during the time of Jesus. Jesus here is emphasizing that the greatness of his ministry, and that of John's, is not found in the pomp and rule of power and subjugation.

Jesus then goes on again, as we have seen elsewhere, to indirectly associate his ministry with that of Yahweh (Luke 7:27), likening John with the forerunner to Yahweh in Malachi 3:1. Jesus then proceeds to discuss the reversal that God's kingdom brings. The great shall be considered small, and vice versa (Luke 7:28). Neither John nor Jesus was what the people expected; neither fit the particular mold of what they had anticipated. The Pharisees and the Jews of Jesus' day believed that if they fulfilled specific

5. Van Aarde, "Silver Coin," 11.

parameters of moral cleanliness or conducted particular rituals, that they could move God to bring forth his kingdom on their terms. But this as empty as children thinking they can create joy through a celebration by merely playing the proper instruments. Or that they can create sadness by merely playing a dirge.

Many subtle layers in Jesus' words deepen our understanding of Jesus' point.[6] First, the children in Luke 7:32 are *sitting*, although they act as if they are indignantly calling other children to play. Second, the children "call them," but this may be more appropriately translated as "address them." They are calling others informally to play, but they are pretending to be formal. Third, "sitting in the marketplace" could also be understood as "sitting in judgment." But clearly, their judgments are childish and shallow.

In the end, all the accomplishments of Jesus' enemies are mockeries of their own efforts. Of course, this is seen supremely in the cross. But the authenticity of Jesus' message is established in its actual accomplishments. True repentance amongst true sinners; the real restoration of real outcasts. Wendy Cotter writes:

> To what then, is this generation compared? It is like children sitting in judgment at the courts, who address their peers, saying, "We piped to you and you did not dance; we wailed and you did not mourn." The parable is designed to expose self-righteousness as so much sham. No matter how "this generation" may convince itself by externals, and by the prestige of office, that it may pronounce judgment due to its supposed wisdom and integrity, its very judgments betray the superficiality it labours to hide.[7]

Real joy comes as a *response* to God's program. Joy is about something to Jesus. It celebrates something concrete. "Wisdom is proved right by all her children" (Luke 7:35). In other words, the way of Jesus will be vindicated by the fruit it bears. When people return to God, when the lost are found, when sinners repent— those are causes for celebration, because they justify God's radical

6. See the discussion by Cotter, "Children in the Market-Place," 289–304.
7. Cotter, "Children in the Market-Place," 302.

program of grace in Jesus. Is God *for* me? Of course. But that is not the decisive way to frame the question. Rather, we could say, "Am I *for* God?" That is, am I ready for him to have his honor. It not only our justification that is at stake, but it is also *his*.

Conclusion

Søren Kierkegaard once told a parable about a king who loved a peasant girl. The king was afraid that if the girl saw him in all his glory, then she would love him for his majesty instead of for himself. He also feared that he might frighten or overwhelm her with power and majesty; consequently, she might not be open to his pursuit. How does the king solve this dilemma? The king chooses to enter the village of ordinary people, *as one of them*, and eventually, through his mundane, persistent love, to win over the peasant girl. Only when he had won her over did he reveal who he truly was, a majestic king.[1]

The parables of Jesus are not so different from this king in disguise. Jesus said that he told parables for a reason. It was to make those who did not want to see even blinder, and those who wanted to see even more clearsighted (Mark 4:1–25). In other words, the parables are meant to draw us into a mystery, to entice us into thinking God's thoughts after him.

In the parables, as in the life of Jesus, remember, *the sacred becomes secular without loss.* Kierkegaard's story helps us here as well. Because the whole concept of God-in-Jesus begs the question, has God in his transcendent "holy, holy, holy" not now changed to become something altogether different? We could ask the same question of Kierkegaard's king. Was it inconsistent with his royal power to enter the fray of common people? Surely not. Is he not free to do so? Surely he is. Does it make him more noble or

---

1. Oden, *Parables of Kierkegaard*, 40–45.

less noble to do so? If anything, it makes him more noble and adds to his character. Perhaps the act of voluntarily lowering his status is, after all, the most regal thing.

What changed? It was not the king's greatness, but only the additional role he took upon himself. The king became a peasant because the king became a *pursuer*. Concerning the incarnation of Yahweh in Jesus, Richard Bauckham writes:

> An important point to make in this connection is that the identity of the God of Israel does not exclude the unexpected and surprising. Quite the contrary, this God's freedom as God requires his freedom from all human expectations, even those based on his revealed identity. He may act in new and surprising ways, in which he proves to be the same God, consistent with his known identity, but in unexpected ways. He is both free and faithful. He is not capricious but nor is he predictable. He may be trusted to be consistent with himself, but he may surprise in the ways he proves consistent with himself.[2]

Ironically, through the earthiness of these parables, we see what might be the greatest facets of God's glory. They are like the stars against the night sky. In light of the lowliness of these stories, we can see and appreciate the greatness of the audacious love of God.

This mystery is compounded, further, by the individual who spoke these parables to us. He was himself that disguised king. As we enter our Ben's Chili Bowl on our Saturday afternoon, we suddenly find ourselves being addressed by someone greater than any president. Jesus broke through the Creator/creation divide to seek sinners. Jesus, as the embodiment of God's temple, in his regal and priestly roles, carried a contagious holiness. We discussed how this was his *life's work*. As a doctor is honored by the recovery of his patient, so Jesus is honored by the return of a lost one.

Further, in the immediate background of Luke 15 is Jesus' specific journey to his cross, which captures in its horror the slave's death that awaited him. Even as he told a set of parables about those who risked it all to find their lost items, Jesus was risking it

2. Bauckham, *God Crucified*, 71.

all for his mission of grace. The result of his mission would be joy as the lost are found, as the world is turned upside down.

In the repentance of a sinner, there are two parties that are justified. The sinner and God himself. What God did in Jesus is not something we can understand. It seems completely counterintuitive. Wasteful and extravagant. Like a permissive father giving away his whole estate to win back his lost children. But this, in some sense, we can relate to. Through Jesus' mission, *God gave his son for us*, while he should perhaps, it seems to us, have justly sacrificed all of creation for his son instead.

As we lastly reflected on the joy of God's celebration, we saw how this joy corresponded with the vindication of God's unconventional program. But there are several expressions of joy in Luke's Gospel that I intentionally neglected. I have saved them to the end as an encouragement for us to consider. These instances are found in the bookends of Luke's Gospel.

The first is the joy in Luke's account of the nativity (Luke 1–2). All the familiar elements are there. The reversal of status—neither Elizabeth nor Zechariah nor Joseph have the greatest honor in this account, although they bear all the markers of honor within their culture: pedigree, old age, and regal/priestly associations (Luke 1:5–7, 27). But Mary, a poor young virgin, is the central voice and focus of Luke's story (Luke 1:26–56; 2:5–7, 16–51).[3] Many verses reflecting the joy of John the Baptist's and Jesus' births surround the text, including Mary's own exclamation (Luke 1:46b–53):

> My soul glorifies the Lord and my spirit rejoices in God my Savior, for he has been mindful of the humble state of his servant. From now on all generations will call me blessed, for the Mighty One has done great things for me—holy is his name. His mercy extends to those who fear him, from generation to generation. He has performed mighty deeds with his arm; he has scattered those who are proud in their inmost thoughts. He has brought down rulers from their thrones but has lifted up

3. For a fuller discussion, see Green, "Social Status of Mary," 457–72.

the humble. He has filled the hungry with good things
but has sent the rich away empty.

Again, the theme of joy and reversal combine with the promise of Jesus, "the Messiah, the Lord" (Luke 2:11). But amid all
the joy is found that grammatic uncertainty so typical of Luke's
Gospel. Mary's response to the angel is, "How will this be?" (Luke
1:34). This, as we discussed earlier, is in the subjunctive mood. The
mood of possibility, chance, risk, amazement. Can it *really* be true?

The second and final occurrence of joy is at the end of the
Gospel of Luke. As Jesus appears to his disciples, having overcome
death, they all experience "joy and amazement" (Luke 24:41;
24:52), but that is not all. Matthew's Gospel appears to describe the
same scene.[4] In Matthew 28:16–17, he records that the disciples
"worshipped; but some doubted." Luke's fuller text in Luke 24:41
reads, "*they still did not believe it* because of joy and amazement"
(emphasis mine). They were literally "unbelieving from joy."

Does God have regard for me? It is hard to believe it. I know.
And that is okay. It does not hinge upon us. Our belief of it is not
what makes it true. We need not believe perfectly to be part of
this kingdom. To be part of this celebration. The Gospel of Luke
has its faithful doubters, does it not? Zechariah, Mary, Peter, even
John the Baptist himself. We need not be afraid to count ourselves
among their number. Remember, it is the father who runs to the
son. It is the father who lays it on the line. We need only to look
up and see that God is not distant. He has already made the journey to our place, and he knows our condition. Perhaps we are lost.
Perhaps that is what we are. But he is still and will always be our
seeker. That is who he is.

4. Licona, *Why Are There Differences?*, 178–80.

Bibliography

Bailey, Kenneth. *The Cross and the Prodigal: Luke 15 through the Eyes of Middle Eastern Peasants.* Downers Grove: InterVarsity, 2005.

———. *Finding the Lost: Cultural Keys to Luke 15.* St. Louis: Concordia, 1992.

———. *The Good Shepherd: A Thousand-Year Journey from Psalm 23 to the New Testament.* Downers Grove: Intervarsity, 2014.

Bauckham, Richard. *God Crucified: Monotheism and Christology in the New Testament.* Grand Rapids: Eerdmans, 1999.

———. *Jesus and the Eyewitnesses: The Gospels as Eyewitness Testimony.* Second edition. Grand Rapids: Eerdmans, 2017.

Bauer, Walter. *A Greek-English Lexicon of the New Testament and Other Early Christian Literature.* 2nd ed. Chicago: University of Chicago Press, 1979.

Blajer, Piotr. "What is the Purpose of the Older Brother in the Parable? A Narrative Study of Luke 15." *Liber Annuus* 67 (2017) 127-49.

Blomberg, Craig L. "The Authenticity and Significance of Jesus' Table Fellowship with Sinners." In *Key Events in the Life of the Historical Jesus: Collaborative Exploration of Context and Coherence,* edited by Darrell L. Bock and Robert L. Webb, 215–50. Grand Rapids: Eerdmans, 2010.

Bock, Darrell L. *A Theology of Luke and Acts.* Grand Rapids: Zondervan, 2015.

Braude, William G. *The Midrash on Psalms.* New Haven: Yale University Press, 1987.

Burke, Trevor J. "The Parable of the Prodigal Father: An Interpretative Key to the Third Gospel (Luke 15:11–32)." *Tyndale Bulletin* 64 (2013) 217–38.

Casey, Patrick J. "A Parable of God's Love for Sinners: Luke 15:11–32." *Calvary Baptist Theological Journal* 5 (1989) 28–42.

Cotter, Wendy J. "The Parable of the Children in the Market-Place, Q (Lk) 7:31–35: An Examination of the Parable's Image and Significance." *Novum Testamentum* 29 (1987) 289–304.

Cox, Kendall. "Karl Barth's Christological Interpretation of Luke 15:11–32." *Journal of Reformed Theology* 13 (2019) 215–37.

Dodd, C. H. *The Parables of the Kingdom.* San Francisco: Harper and Row, 1981.

Donahue, John R. *The Gospel in Parable: Metaphor, Narrative, and Theology in the Synoptic Gospels.* Philadelphia: Fortress, 1988.

Bibliography

Doole, J. Andrew. "Observational Comedy in Luke 15." *Neotestamentica* 50 (2016) 181–209.

Downing, Gerald F. "Redaction Criticism: Antiquities and the Synoptic Gospels (II)." *Journal for the Study of the New Testament* 2 (1980) 46–65.

Dykstra, Robert C. "Finding Ourselves Lost." *Pastoral Psychology* 59 (2010) 737–46.

Eng, Daniel. "The Widening Circle: Honour, Shame, and Collectivism in the Parable of the Prodigal Son." *Expository Times* 130.5 (2019) 193–201.

Finney, Mark T. "*Servile Supplicium*: Shame and the Deuteronomic Curse— Crucifixion in Its Cultural Context." *Biblical Theology Bulletin* 43 (2013) 124–34.

Fletcher-Louis, Crispin. "Jesus as the High Priestly Messiah: Part 1." *Journal for the Study of the Historical Jesus* 4.2 (2006) 155–75.

———. "Jesus as the High Priestly Messiah: Part 2." *Journal for the Study of the Historical Jesus* 5.1 (2007) 57–79.

Gathercole, Simon. *The Preexistent Son: Recovering the Christologies of Matthew, Mark, and Luke*. Grand Rapids: Eerdmans, 2006.

George, Mark K. "Yhwh's Own Heart." *Catholic Biblical Quarterly* 64 (2002) 442–59.

Gibson, J. "Hoi Telōnai kai hai Pornai." *Journal of Theological Studies* 32.3 (1981) 429–33.

Goodacre, Mark S. *The Synoptic Problem: A Way Through the Maze*. London: Sheffield Academic Press, 2001.

Green, Joel B. *The Gospel of Luke*. Grand Rapids: Eerdmans, 1997.

———. "The Social Status of Mary in Luke 1,5-2,52: A Plea for Methodological Integration." Biblica 73 (1992) 457-72.

Häkkinen, Sakari. "Poverty in the First-century Galilee." *HTS Theological Studies*, 72.4 (2016) 1–9.

Hamm, Dennis. "What the Samaritan Leper Sees: The Narrative Christology of Luke 17:11–19." *Catholic Biblical Quarterly* 56.2 (1994) 273–87.

Harrill, J. Albert. "The Indentured Labor of the Prodigal Son (Luke 15:15)." *Journal of Biblical Literature* 115.4 (1996) 714–17.

Harrington, Hannah K. "Did the Pharisees Eat Ordinary Food in a State of Ritual Purity?" *Journal for the Study of Judaism in the Persian, Hellenistic, and Roman Period* 26.1 (1995) 42–54.

Hays, Richard B. "Netted." In *The Art of Reading Scripture*, edited by Ellen F. Davis and Richard B. Hays, 311–16. Grand Rapids: Eerdmans, 2003.

Holland, Tom. *Dominion: How the Christian Revolution Remade the World*. New York: Basic, 2019.

Hultgren, Arland J. *The Parables of Jesus: A Commentary*. Grand Rapids: Eerdmans, 2000.

Jarvis, Cynthia A. "Ministry in the Subjunctive Mood." *Theology Today* 66.4 (2010) 445–58.

Josephus, Flavius. *The Works of Flavius Josephus*. Translated by William Whiston. Buffalo: John E. Beardsley, 1895.

Bibliography

Kilgallen, John. "Was Jesus Right to Eat with Sinners and Tax Collectors?" *Biblica* 93.4 (2012) 590–600.

Levenson, Jon D. "The Temple and the World." *Journal of Religion* 64.3 (1984) 275–98.

Levine, Amy-Jill. *Short Stories by Jesus: The Enigmatic Parables of a Controversial Rabbi*. New York: HarperOne, 2014.

Licona, Michael. *Why Are There Differences in the Gospels? What We Can Learn From Ancient Biography*. New York: Oxford University Press, 2017.

MacArthur, John. "An Extraordinary Celebration." Crossmap Blogs, May 17, 2021. https://blogs.crossmap.com/2021/05/17/an-extraordinary-celebration/.

———. *The Prodigal Son: An Astonishing Study of the Parable Jesus Told to Unveil God's Grace for You*. Nashville: Thomas Nelson, 2008.

Marcus, Joel. "Crucifixion as Parodic Exaltation." *Journal of Biblical Literature* 125.1 (2006) 73–87.

Menken, Maarten J. J. "The Position of Σπλαγχνίζεσθαι and Σπλάγχνα in the Gospel of Luke." *Novum Testamentum* 30.2 (1988) 107–14.

Neusner, Jacob. *The Pharisees: Rabbinic Perspectives*. Hoboken, NJ: Ktav, 1983.

Notley, Steven R. "The Sea of Galilee: Development of an Early Christian Toponym." *Journal of Biblical Literature* 183 (2009) 183–88.

Oden, Thomas C. *Parables of Kierkegaard*. Princeton: Princeton University Press, 1978.

Reed, Jonathan L. "Instability in Jesus' Galilee: A Demographic Perspective." *Journal of Biblical Literature* 129.2 (2010) 343–65.

Rindge, Matthew S. "Luke's Artistic Parables: Narratives of Subversion, Imagination, and Transformation." *Interpretation* 64 (2014) 403–15.

Saldarini, Anthony J. *Pharisees, Scribes, and Sadducees in Palestinian Society: A Sociological Approach*. Grand Rapids: Eerdmans, 2001.

Sanders, E. P. "Jesus and the Sinners." *Journal for the Study of the New Testament* 19 (1983) 5–36.

Scott, Bernard Brandon. "Heroes From on High." *The Anglican Theological Review* 69.2 (1987) 135–44.

Seamands, Stephen A. "An Inclusive Vision of the Holy Life." *Asbury Theological Journal* 42 (1987) 79–88.

Sellew, Philip. "Interior Monologue as a Narrative Device in the Parables of Luke." *Journal of Biblical Literature* 111 (1992) 239–53.

Snodgrass, Klyne. *Stories with Intent: A Comprehensive Guide to the Parables of Jesus*. Grand Rapids: Eerdmans, 2018.

Sproul, R. C. *The Holiness of God*. Stream, IL: Tyndale House, 1998.

Spurgeon, Charles Haddon. "The Approachableness of Jesus." Metropolitan Tabernacle Pulpit Volume 14, n.d. https://www.spurgeon.org/resource-library/sermons/the-approachableness-of-jesus.

Stagg, Frank. "Luke's Theological Use of Parables." *Review and Expositor* 94 (1997) 215–29.

Stettler, Hanna. *Heiligung bei Paulus: ein Beitrag aus biblisch-theologischer Sicht*. Tübingen: Mohr Siebeck, 2014.

Bibliography

Stonehouse, Ned Bernard. *J. Gresham Machen: A Biographical Memoir.* Edinburgh: Banner of Truth, 1987.

Szkredka, Sławomir. "The Call of Simon Peter in Luke 5:1–11: A Lukan Invention?" *The Biblical Annals* 8 (2018) 173–89.

Taylor, Vincent. *The Passion Narrative of St. Luke: A Critical and Historical Investigation.* Cambridge: Cambridge University Press, 1972.

Tozer, A. W. *Knowledge of the Holy.* Harrisburg, PA: Christian Publications, 1961.

van Aarde, A. G. "A Silver Coin in the Mouth of a Fish (Matthew 17:24–27)— A Miracle of Nature, Economy, Ecology and the Politics of Holiness." *Neotestamentica* 27 (1993) 1–25.

van de Weghe, Luuk. "Acts 27–28: The Cerebral Scars of Shipwreck." *Tyndale Bulletin* 70.2 (2019) 205–20.

———. "The Beloved Eyewitness." *New Testament Studies* 66 (2022) 351–57.

———. "Early Divine Christology: Scripture, Narrativity and Confession in Luke-Acts." In *Scripture and Theology: Historical and Systematic Perspectives*, edited by Tomas Bokedal, Ludger Jansen, and M. Borowski. Berlin: De Gruyter, 2023.

———. "Name Recall in the Synoptic Gospels." *New Testament Studies* 69.1 (2022) 95–109.

———. *The Historical Tell: Patterns of Eyewitness Testimony in the Gospel of Luke and Acts.* Chillicothe, OH: DeWard, 2023.

van Eck, Ernest. "In the Kingdom Everybody Has Enough—A Social-Scientific and Realistic Reading of the Parable of the Lost Sheep (Lk 15:4–6)." *HTS Theological Studies* 67 (2011) 1–10.

———. *The Parables of Jesus the Galilean: Stories of a Social Prophet.* Eugene, OR: Wipf and Stock, 2016.

———. "A Realistic Reading of the Parable of the Lost Coin in Q: Gaining or Losing Even More?" *HTS Theological Studies* 75 (2019) 1–9.

Vearncombe, Erin K. "Searching for a Lost Coin: Papyrological Backgrounds for Q 15, 8–10." In *Metaphor, Narrative, and Parables in Q*, edited by Dieter Roth, Ruben Zimmerman, and Michael Labahn, 307–37. Wissenschaftliche Untersuchungenzum Neuen Testament 315. Tübingen: Mohr Siebeck, 2014.

Wassen, Cecilia. "Jesus' Table Fellowship with 'Toll Collectors and Sinners.'" *Journal for the Study of the Historical Jesus* 14 (2016) 137–57.

Wendland, Ernst R. "Finding Some Lost Aspects of Meaning in Christ's Parables of the Lost—and Found (Luke 15)." *Trinity Journal* 17 (1996) 19–65.

Wilder, Amos N. *The Language of the Gospel: Early Christian Rhetoric.* New York: Harper and Row, 1964.

Yinger, Kent L. *The Pharisees: Their History, Character, and New Testament Portrait.* Eugene, OR: Cascade, 2022.

Young, Brad H. *The Parables: Jewish Tradition and Christian Interpretation.* Grand Rapids: Baker, 2008.

Young, Vershawn Ashanti. "'Nah, We Straight': An Argument against Code Switching." *Journal of Applied Communications* 29.1 (2009) 49–76.

Index

Index